Graphic Design
BASICS

Marketing &
Promoting
Your Work

Maria Piscopo

NORTH LIGHT BOOKS

Cincinnati, Ohio

This hardcover edition of *Marketing & Promoting Your Work* features a "self-jacket" that eliminates the need for a separate dust jacket. It provides sturdy protection for your book while it saves paper, trees and energy.

Other fine North Light Books are available from your local bookstore, art supply store or direct from the publisher.

99 98 97 96 95   5 4 3 2 1

Library of Congress Cataloging-in-Publication Data

Piscopo, Maria
    Marketing & promoting your work / by Maria Piscopo.—1st ed.
      p.   cm—(Graphic design basics)
    Includes index.
    ISBN 0-89134-608-2
    1. Graphic arts—United States—Marketing. I. Title. II. Series.
NC1001.P57   1995
741.6'068'8—dc20

Edited by Diana Martin
Designed by Angela Lennert
Cover illustration by Angela Lennert

The permissions on page v constitute an extension of this copyright page.

METRIC CONVERSION CHART

TO CONVERT	TO	MULTIPLY BY
Inches	Centimeters	2.54
Centimeters	Inches	0.4
Feet	Centimeters	30.5
Centimeters	Feet	0.03
Yards	Meters	0.9
Meters	Yards	1.1
Sq. Inches	Sq. Centimeters	6.45
Sq. Centimeters	Sq. Inches	0.16
Sq. Feet	Sq. Meters	0.09
Sq. Meters	Sq. Feet	10.8
Sq. Yards	Sq. Meters	0.8
Sq. Meters	Sq. Yards	1.2
Pounds	Kilograms	0.45
Kilograms	Pounds	2.2
Ounces	Grams	28.4
Grams	Ounces	0.04

I would like to thank my agent, Mike Hamilburg, for always making these books happen for me and Cindy Brennemen for all her hard work managing and producing my lecture and workshop tours.

Special thanks to my family, Frank and Frances Piscopo, Charles and Denise Piscopo and Roseanne and Chuck Mitchell for their love and support.

Eternal gratitude to the Howard Family in Gold Bar for all their prayers.

I also want to thank Bob, Mary and Shadow for the much needed rest and recreation from walking the dog.

This book is dedicated to the next generation, half these kids are destined to become successful and talented artists and will use this book: Danielle, Meghan, Nathan, Maranda, Graham, Desiree, Heather, Jacob, Michael Loy, Andrew, Gregory, Natalie and Spencer.

About the Author

Maria Piscopo has been a creative services consultant for the past fifteen years. Her seminars and workshops have helped thousands of companies change the way they do business, increasing their bottom line. She has conducted in-house training sessions for AT&T, National Geographic Television and Teledyne CAE, among others. Maria is a popular speaker at conferences and is the author of books and audio and video cassettes geared for increasing productivity and profitability.

Her articles have been published in national and international magazines, including *HOW*, *Step-By-Step Graphics*, *NADTP Journal* and *Communication Arts*. She currently teaches for the Dynamic Graphics Educational Foundation and the Art Center College of Design. Maria is a past president of Visual Artists Association and Women in Management and is active in many industry associations.

Permissions

Contents

professionalism, expertise and ability to stay within budgets and meet deadlines. Find out how to be smart abut expenses, changes/revisions, deposits, billing and cancellation charges.

Chapter Five: Getting Repeat Business

Chapter Six: Managing Conflict

Chapter Seven: Hiring Professional Services

Chapter Eight: Planning for Action

Gallery

Browse through more promotional pieces and strategic insights that prove how smart planning and a commitment to marketing pay off.

Index

Super Strategy List

SUPER STRATEGIES

Throughout this book you will find special tips and advice about promoting your work successfully. They will appear in boxes just like this. These "Super Strategies" will help you save time, create more effective promotional campaigns and get you more of the kind of design work you want to do.

Introduction

In school we are taught all about the creative and technical aspects of being a graphic artist, but what about this business of selling yourself? I first got involved in business education for creative professionals as a member of the advisory council at Orange Cost College. When asked what could be done to improve the program for photography and graphic arts students, several of us responded, "Teach business skills."

Although students of the arts could take business and marketing classes in another department of the college, they often did not. A class was needed that addressed the many aspects creative professionals need to be successful, that could not be covered in a regular business class. Those of us on the advisory council felt that teaching business practices would not only improve a student's chance for success, but would also raise the level of professionalism of our industry.

I was invited to submit a class proposal, and after its acceptance by the curriculum committee, and with the tremendous support and assistance of Assistant Dean Rick Steadry, I began teaching a business practices class. My goal was to prepare students to start businesses and market themselves successfully as creative professionals. Teaching the class led to my giving seminar programs and writing articles on the subject of marketing creative services.

With this book, my goal is to concentrate on the marketing aspects of a graphic design business. This is a "how-to" book with many different ideas you can put into practice. It doesn't matter what your level of experience is. If you're just starting out, you'll save time, money and energy by beginning with a plan of action for the promotion of your business. If you have been in business a few years and are surviving by word-of-mouth, you can take control of your future by implementing a solid marketing strategy. If you have a promotion plan, but have not been happy with the results— if you want bigger, better clients— you will learn techniques to fine tune your promotion which will in turn allow you to achieve your goals.

Because time is always at a pre- mium for creative professionals, you'll find ideas in this book you can use to incorporate promotion into your daily work schedule. Money is also an important consideration in promoting your business—you'll need to plan on spending some. Put aside between 5 and 10 percent of your annual gross sales to cover promotional expenses. Another thing you'll need is a lot of patience. Building a successful business takes more than an overnight effort. I recommend a marketing strategy that covers at least twelve months in order to give your plan a chance to succeed.

Many people ask me if my marketing techniques and ideas work. My reply always is "Only if you do!" Success comes before work only in the dictionary, never in real life. It takes time, money and patience to accomplish your goals. Setting goals will be a key to your success. Spending resources without written goals is like trying to reach an unknown destination without a map. You'll get places a lot faster if you know where you're going and have some idea of what path to take to get there.

Marketing and Promoting Yo

1

Yes! You can do it all.

STEP ONE
Target your market(s).

STEP TWO
Find the time to do it.

2

Getting the word out.

STEP ONE
Make good use of direct mail.

STEP TWO
Advertise your services.

STEP THREE
Toot your own horn.

3

Making contact.

STEP ONE
Set up a mediabase.

STEP TWO
Research new clients.

STEP THREE
Identify the contact person.

STEP FOUR
Make the big call.

STEP FIVE
Present your portfolio.

4

Working with clients.

STEP ONE
Understand the client/ designer relationship.

STEP TWO
Set the right tone for pricing.

STEP THREE
Show what the project is worth.

ur Work From Start to Finish

5

Getting repeat business.

STEP ONE
Make your clients
want to stay.

STEP TWO
Use business building
techniques.

STEP THREE
Learn to work with
out-of-town clients.

6

Managing conflict.

STEP ONE
Sell your ideas to
the client.

STEP TWO
Turn problem clients into
profitable clients.

7

Hiring professional
services.

STEP ONE
Determine if you
need a rep.

STEP TWO
Find the right rep.

STEP THREE
Hire a marketing
coordinator.

8

Planning for action.

STEP ONE
Pull the pieces of your plan together.

STEP TWO
Lay out each and every action.

STEP THREE
Match action to objective.

STEP FOUR
Integrate your plan and daily calendar.

Chapter One
Yes! You Can Do It All!

S T E P   O N E

Target your markets.

●

S T E P   T W O

Find the time to do it.

Like most designers, you probably started your business on a "word of mouth" basis with jobs coming from referrals. Now, though, you have started thinking about the direction and focus of your business. Do you have a direction? A focus? Are they the right ones? This chapter will help you find or clarify that focus and set short- and long-term goals for your design business. It will help you learn to target specific markets for your design services by style, industry and usage and help you find the time to build good relationships with your clients.

STEP 1 Target Your Markets

To become and remain a profitable and recession-proof business, it is important to develop *multiple profit centers* or sources of new business. Each profit center is the result of a different target market and marketing message. It is normal business practice to target more than one market for your services. It's the old question, "Are you a specialist or a generalist?" The answer, both! Ultimately, clients will hire the specialist in order to get exactly what they need. It is the "safe" way for most clients. Once they are comfortable and happy with the designer, they will use that person or firm for a variety of projects. So, to become a generalist, that is, all things to your current clients, you must start out as a specialist with one focused marketing message to your prospective clients.

It is important to treat current clients and prospective clients differently. In order to target new markets for your work, first answer these questions: Do you want to do more of the same work, but for better clients with bigger budgets? Or, do you want to do different types of design projects?

Targeting Techniques

There are three ways to target markets for design services.

1. By style

It takes a very secure client to go with your personal style to sell his product or service instead of taking the safe, conservative route! But, if your style is one of your biggest sales assets, consider this approach. Selling style tends to be used by high-end clients or clients in cutting edge industries. When you target a specific style, philosophy, or approach to design, your prospective client base will be broad, as you can see in the diagram below.

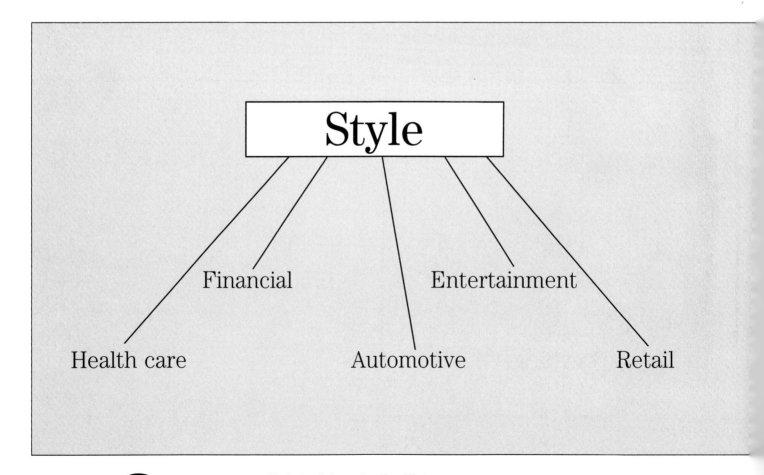

Style

Financial   Entertainment

Health care   Automotive   Retail

2. By industry

This is probably the most common type of targeting because it is so easy to identify clients. Almost all resource books are organized by industry or standard industrial classification codes. If you decide to target a specific industry, the potential profit centers will be the various uses of your design services, as you can see from the diagram below.

Don't focus on just newsletters; you may be overlooking many other prospective design opportunities. Once you have done work for a particular industry, for example, a financial firm, you can sell your experience and expertise in the industry to other financial companies.

3. By usage

Let's say that you really enjoy packaging design and want a major profit center to be in this area. Specific targeting such as this works well because it helps you identify client categories. For example, industries that use packaging design include food, pharmaceutical and beauty products. Just visit your favorite grocery store and see how large a specific-usage category can be.

When developing your target markets, it is extremely important that you use the targeting technique that offers you the broadest possible client base.

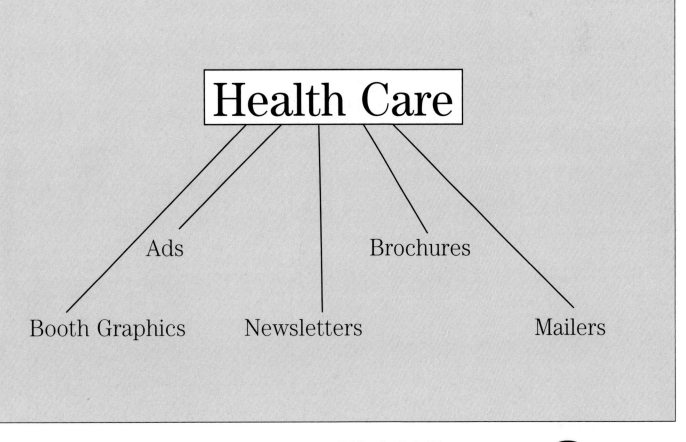

SUPER STRATEGY

ONE

Build Good Relations

"I have built my business primarily through building good relations with my clients. I have always tried to establish long-term relationships. It is more important for me to establish a relationship than it is to make as much money as possible from each individual job. Most clients are interested in a long-term relationship. Build up trust and you will keep clients over the long haul. Getting into each other's head is crucial. This gives me freedom to try things without having to worry about what they like. I want an intuitive relationship with my clients.

"Long-term relationships come down to reliability. Clients know they are going to get a good job, more than what they need. They need things in a hurry. They can hand projects over to me and get something they can be proud of in return. I make my clients look good. I am also a calming influence.

"The majority of work I get is through referrals. So my clients are not only a source of work but also a potential source for new clients. I have been able to network within companies (Cahners, BOMC, Price Waterhouse) and between companies through these relationships.

"I have also made it a point to target entrepreneurs or start-up companies. Though this can be risky and somewhat demanding, I see the benefits as twofold. First, I can grow with their company. Second, they are more apt to give me bigger projects and more responsibility than a larger company would."

Michael Pilla
Michael Pilla Design

STEP 2 Find the Time to Do It

How does it feel to be the chief of new business development as well as the head of your own creative department? Do you wonder how you'll find the time and means to do it all well? As a one-person shop, you wear all the hats. So, here are five keys to creating and promoting at the same time. When marketing works, and new business comes in, these keys will help you avoid the tendency to wind down and lose your momentum. Otherwise, when your business slows down, you'll face the downside of the "feast or famine" syndrome.

Take a "Business First" Attitude.

Understand that you are first a businessperson, then a designer. If you have recently said to yourself, "All I really want to do is be a designer," you need to review your attitude about self-employment and consider a staff job.

Plan for Success; Don't Wait for It to Happen

You need to get goals, not just set them. The key to successful goal achievement is to *write it down*. Your subconscious simply does not recognize the unwritten goal. Putting your desires onto paper (or floppy disk) creates an unrestricted flow of energy and dedication to achieving those goals. In chapter eight, you'll find sample "action plans" of specific goal-getting for new business development.

Stay Motivated

Staying motivated day after day to do it all—the marketing and the creating—takes an assertive attitude. You may already be doing this and not have identified that you have taken a position on the subject! But if you find yourself tossed around from job to job or client to client and losing your direction and motivation, you may need an attitude check! Take the Self-Diagnostic Attitude Test on page 11 and see.

Manage Stress; Don't Let It Manage You

Most stress in a design business comes from trying to balance conflicting needs. You need to be businesslike and you want to be creative. You need to dedicate yourself to your work and you want to spend time with your family. Sound familiar? You probably could write an endless list of personal and professional stressful situations. The important thing is to accept that this stress is normal. Distress, such as family illness or natural disasters, however, is not the norm and can't be managed like stress can be. But, if you have determined that you are dealing with stress and not distress, try these simple rules:

- **You'll never catch up on all your re-**sponsibilities, so stop trying. There will always be a never-ending succession of business, marketing and design tasks to do. Stop waiting for the in-basket to be empty. Stop waiting to arrive; start enjoying the journey!

- **Don't expect to make everyone happy.** There will always be a design client who wants you to feel or behave differently (especially with pricing). Stop expecting people to always approve of you or be happy with you. You can only do your very best to please your clients *and* run a profitable business. You can't control other people's feelings about you.

- **Learn to say "NO."** Stress is created when you say "yes" when all logic and common sense tells you to say "no." Pricing a design job is a perfect example. A client makes an assignment or pricing request and you *know* that an unqualified "yes" will cause great stress (and reduced profits). Since you can't walk around saying "no!" to clients and stay in business, here are three stress-reducing options: "No, *but* here's another way to do that"; "Yes, *and* this is what that change will cost"; "I'll get back to you" (this buys time to create a solution).

Find More Time

You know that any activity expands to fill the time given to it. So, unless

Find the Time to Do It

otherwise managed, your day will fill up with "things to do" other than marketing your work. Because of this, you want to know where to find the time to do everything you *need* to do (marketing) and *want* to do (great jobs for your clients). The time is there. All you have to do is *uncover* it. Time can be buried in many different ways. Do any of these sound familiar?

• You give priority to tasks that are agreeable and then have no time left to do the less enjoyable but necessary chores because your day is "full."

• You give priority to tasks that are easy—different side of the same problem. By doing all the easy things first, you bury the time for the bigger and harder jobs because you are waiting to "find" the time.

• It's here—you do whatever is in front of you without regard to priority or level of importance. Half the day is "gone" and you don't know where it went.

Now that you are aware of how you hide time, use some of that time to read the sidebar on page 12 to learn how to uncover it.

How to Manage Stress
(aka How to Succeed as a Businessperson)

1. Accept that you will never get everything done that you'd like to.

2. Accept that you will never make everyone happy.

3. Learn how to say "no."

4. Reprioritize tasks and don't sweat the ones at the bottom of the list that don't get done.

5. Reprioritize how you use your time.

6. Stress to friends and family that office hours are sacred—don't call unless they want to hire you!

7. Don't disregard your health and mental well-being. Don't give up workouts or walks. Don't forget to stop and play with your cats occasionally.

8. Visit the library for a good thriller or mystery so you always have a book to read in the evenings to take your mind off work.

9. Take up a hobby, such as fly-fishing, that forces you out of the office.

10. Try to enter your office each morning with renewed strength and resilience. Let yourself realize how much you enjoy being your own boss!

Marketing & Promoting Your Work

Self-Diagnostic Attitude Test

If you find yourself floundering in uncertainties and other new businessperson maladies, take a minute to complete this brief test.

1. Are You Acting Confidently?
☐ Yes
☐ No
Successful businesspeople all have one thing in common: a very strong, calm sense of confidence. This confidence is made, not born.

2. Is Fear Stopping You?
☐ Yes
☐ No
Motivation comes from testing yourself and passing the tests. The most important thing to know is that *you must not wait* for fears to subside so you can be motivated. You could wait forever! It turns out that your feelings follow your behavior. *Acting* confidently will eventually help you overcome fear and create confidence and motivation. Don't wait to overcome doubt and fear before facing any professional challenge. Accept that they are part of the process of testing and winning.

3. Do You Feel Alone in Your Fears and Anxieties?
☐ Yes
☐ No
Negative and demotivating feelings are indicators that you are doing something you haven't done before—that's all! Most new entrepreneurs experience them. The lack of motivation and confidence comes from the lack of practice. For example, the first time you quote a really big job or tell a client they can't get the job by the day they want it, you will feel some fear and anxiety. Don't worry; you are experiencing a perfectly normal reaction any business owner feels when being assertive. Acting assertively may cause you some short-term discomfort, but it will deliver long-term motivation, satisfaction and confidence. The trick, of course, is to learn to accept the negative feelings rather than waiting for them to go away, and to go on with the work at hand.

Find the Time to Do It

How to Uncover Wasted Time

The tips below are designed so you handle everything only once. This will not only help you find more time, but will do two other things important for a successful design business. One, instead of waiting to find the time for marketing and management (and you never will), they simply become daily scheduled chores. Two, instead of getting depressed because you have a blank calendar, you will always have something on your calendar to work on that will help you move toward success.

1. Transfer every item from your marketing plan (see chapter eight) onto your daily calendar. Make each task specific and "bite-sized" and be sure to allow enough time. Do you know how long it takes to pay bills? Process the daily mail? Write a media release? You'll quickly find out. Don't forget vacations and holidays! Then, use this calendar. Don't be distracted from it by lower-priority tasks.

2. Do you find yourself diverging from priority matters to take unscheduled, noncritical phone calls or being interrupted by nonclients who drop in? Handle these time interlopers only if you can do so immediately and completely. Otherwise, schedule an appointment for them. For example, your best client calls you to request a new brochure, and they want "something different." Rather than drop what you are doing that moment, ask to meet your client at a mutually convenient time and use your daily calendar to schedule the appointment. Everything goes on the calendar. No more lists of things to do!

3. Now, take some of your newly found time to create an important time-finding tool to use with your calendar. Organize thirty-one folders numbered one through thirty-one, one for each day of the month. Then, as you schedule meetings, calls, etc., file all relevant information in the appropriate day file. For example, if July 30 works great for a client meeting, mark your calendar and put related information labeled with the client's name in a file numbered "30." No more piles of paper! No more time wasted looking for information.

SUPER STRATEGY

T W O

Present Yourself Powerfully

"We have done several mailings with our 'Paradigms' brochure. Our advice to designers is don't think about clients. Think about *who you are* and present yourself in a very powerful way. Our brochure evokes a very strong response among clients. They often ask us to 'do for me what you did for yourself.' Our surprise was the sense of trust this piece cultivated in our clients.

"Go in on a call ... if they have your brochure, it's not a cold call. It seems like you have met them before. We have gotten a 6 to 20 percent response rate by sending the piece out to small targeted groups."

Lynn Donham
Church Street Design

AS A CHILD I LOVED WORDS AND PICTURES. GROWING UP I WANTED TO BE A WRITER AND AN ARTIST, BUT I WAS TOLD I HAD TO PICK ONE. GOETHE SAID, "WHATEVER YOU CAN DO OR DREAM YOU CAN, BEGIN IT. BOLDNESS HAS GENIUS, POWER AND MAGIC IN IT." SO I DID. CHURCH STREET DESIGN USES ALL OF WHO I AM. WE CHANNEL INFORMATION AND TECHNOLOGY TO OPEN **DOORWAYS TO NEW IDEAS.** OUR WORDS AND PICTURES WORK TOGETHER. THEY ARE INSEPARABLE. EARNING A LIVING WITH MY IMAGINATION CREATES RISK AND EXCITEMENT. I STILL LOVE WORDS AND PICTURES. I'M GLAD I NEVER CHOSE ONE OR THE OTHER.

In the beginning, words were pictures ...

I HAVE ALWAYS BEEN QUIET. A LISTENER. LISTENING TAKES ME TO THE HEART OF THE MATTER. STANDING ON THE OUTSIDE I CAN LOOK WITHIN. FINDING THE NUANCES, NOTICING THE PATTERNS, MAKING THE CONNECTIONS – THE VISION APPEARS. THROUGH THESE DISCOVERIES I CAN INFORM. I CAN PERSUADE. I CAN DELIGHT. GRAPHIC DESIGN ALLOWS ME TO **MAKE THE VISION REAL.** SO I STAND AT THE WINDOW, QUIETLY. DETERMINED TO LISTEN – AND TO SEE EVERYTHING CLEARLY.

MORE THAN ANYTHING ELSE I ENJOY MAKING THINGS WORK. MEETING THE CHALLENGE. DOING THE IMPOSSIBLE. MAYBE THAT'S WHY I ENJOY PERFORMING MAGIC. I'VE SPENT MANY YEARS LEARNING SLEIGHT OF HAND AND THE ART OF MAGIC. THE CRAFT IS SECOND NATURE TO ME. I LIKE THE SENSE OF MYSTERY AND ENTERTAINMENT, BUT IT'S THE AUDIENCE RESPONSE THAT I FIND MOST GRATIFYING. IN A WAY, GRAPHIC DESIGN IS VERY MAGICAL. MAKING SOMETHING FROM NOTHING. SOLVING PROBLEMS. MAKING IT ALL COME TOGETHER. IF IT ALL WORKS. IF IT'S GOOD COMMUNICATION, I FEEL LIKE I'VE PULLED THE PROVERBIAL RABBIT FROM THE HAT. **APPLAUSE.**

Create Basic Promotion

Once you have decided on your business and marketing goals, you need to create a basic promotion package consisting of identity and promotional pieces to support these goals. Here is how to create a successful promotion package.

1. Develop a logo or identity. Your marketing direction should be reflected in your logo and identity. To illustrate this concept, a designer going after advertising and entertainment industry clients would have an identity with more flair and drama than a designer interested in pursuing banking industry clients. Don't be afraid to put your personality into your logo. This will allow you to attract clients that can identify with your style.

The six elements of a successful identity package and logo application include business cards, letterhead, business envelopes, notepaper, shipping labels, and logo-only labels. These are more elements than the traditional letterhead, business card and envelope package because of the complexity of marketing plans used to sell design today. With today's basic promotion tools, it is better to use simple and inexpensive design solutions in order to get better coverage out of your marketing budget. In other words, don't spend all of your money on a single element.

For example, notepaper printed with your logo can be used for supplemental correspondence and greatly expands your marketing opportunities beyond the traditional business letter. Your logo on a shipping label advertises your design services every time you deliver or mail to clients. The labels with just your logo can be used to customize a report cover for presentations and/or cost proposals. In addition, you will use labels on the back side of your clients' printed work to identify it as your design.

2. Develop multiple uses for your package. Once you have created your identity package, you can then plan additional presentation and promotional uses for it.

Your business card can be added to blank card stock that includes a die cut for it. You can find blank card stock already die cut and ready for card insertion in the wedding announcement section of your local paper warehouse. The combination of the business card and these note cards creates an additional correspondence tool. I use them for following up on portfolio presentations and as thank-you cards for job referrals.

Letterhead can also be used for your client estimates, client invoices, portfolio delivery memos, media releases, capabilities data sheets and, of course, all formal correspondence.

Be sure to print enough business-sized envelopes to cover the use of both your letterhead and the smaller size notepaper correspondence. In other words, if you print 1,000 letterhead and 1,000 notepapers, be sure to print 2,000 envelopes.

The notepaper-sized version of your letterhead can be used in a variety of ways. The note alone in an envelope can be an informal and easy way of saying thank-you for a referral, or the notepaper can be paper clipped to a proposal package with a handwritten, personal note. You can even make notepads and give them to your clients.

In addition to using labels for shipping and mailing, you can use them to personalize promotional material or delivery of artwork. Be careful of post office regulations when designing shipping labels and the placement of your logo in relation to the address area. They don't want to see anything below the zip code.

Don't forget to use your logo label on all presentation materials to both prospective and existing clients.

3. Develop your promotional pieces. These are the more traditional and visual materials used most often to get appointments or to remind clients about your services. They can be inexpensively produced. For example,

Packages

you can mount photographic prints or brochure samples to card stock when you have either a very small target audience or very little money.

With an audience larger than 500, you may want to invest in printed promotional materials. Categories include miniportfolios, capabilities brochures, copy-only or information inserts, newsletters, co-op materials and samples of printed pieces you have designed for your clients.

Miniportfolios are those you would normally show in person, but they are in a format the client can keep. Whether the format is slides, a cover folder with inserts, spiral- or plastic comb-bound pages, or a printed book, the key to its effectiveness is in the concept and design. Keep in mind, clients will often use your miniportfolio to present your work to their own clients or upper management. Quality is vital.

The capabilities brochure concept and design will vary depending on your target market. A low-end target audience that does not pay a high rate for design services should get a less expensive piece than a high-end target audience that pays a higher rate and is in a more competitive market place.

Whether these promo pieces are one-color, one-side 8½″ × 11″ data sheets or four-color brochures, they should include the following: a marketing message, your personal background, facilities information, client testimonials, and a client list or references. Once printed, they can be included in everything from cost proposals to follow-up mailings.

Copy-only or information sheets are wonderful supplements to any promo piece that shows off your design capability. Most designers simply print the information on their letterhead in order to keep costs down. Examples include: a map to your design studio, moving announcements, or information on expansion of services or a current project.

Newsletters have always been labor-intensive promotional pieces. But with the current desktop publishing and digital technology, this process can be simplified and streamlined. Content should include new clients, current project information, personnel changes, and pro bono project news in addition to high-quality information that clients can use. Each newsletter should always include a return response card or enclosure for clients to request more information.

Co-op materials are created by combining the talents of a team of noncompeting creative professionals. This has always been a popular method for promoting design services. However, be careful when using this approach. These materials take time to complete because of the number of people involved, and, normally, you will not be allotted enough room to promote all of your capabilities. Therefore, don't plan on co-op materials to satisfy all of your promotional needs.

A final promotional consideration is the use of samples of printed pieces you have designed for your clients. Using work you have designed for other clients gives you more credibility with prospective clients. This is also a cost-effective technique, because often these are pieces you cannot afford to produce on your own.

There are four ways to adapt these client samples for your promotional use: (a) simply add your logo label and phone number on the front or back cover; (b) print your own advertising message on the back side of single-sided data sheets or ad reprints; (c) design an inexpensive promotional cover and use client samples as inserts; and (d) offer in your direct mail campaigns a portfolio of sample pieces you have designed for your clients.

Once you have produced your basic promotional package, promotions such as advertising, direct mail and public relations are the next step. With these three basic promotion foundations in place, specialty advertising is the next area you should consider.

Idea Jogger

Specialty Advertising Items

These are useful giveaway products customized to feature your company name, logo, and even marketing messages. The object of specialty advertising is name recognition. You are not soliciting a specific action, as you might with advertising or direct mail. There are two kinds of specialty advertising items. The first kind is a simple reminder of your services and is mailed or given to all clients and prospects. The second kind is the premium-use gift which is not given out to all your business contacts. Premium use means that the client has purchased a certain level of services and therefore has earned a premium specialty advertising item.

Specialty Advertising Reminder Items

1. Think in terms of your client or prospect's daily office life. The most traditional reminder item is the classic ceramic mug, customized with your company's name, logo and message.

2. The message on your coffee mugs can be enhanced with custom-printed coasters. These items are sure to keep your name in front of existing and prospective clients every day.

3. The next most traditional customized giveaway is the pen or pencil

specialty item. Be creative. Think about what your clients use on a daily basis. Maybe customized highlighters would keep your name around better than pens or pencils.

4. Specialty paper items, such as customized self-stick notes or the notepads mentioned earlier, are always appreciated by busy clients.

5. Then there are the customized office accessories you can distribute, such as calendars, rulers, magnet clips, paper clip holders, computer mouse pads, staple removers, letter openers, quick slitters (razor blades mounted in durable plastic holders), notepad holders, business card holders, and inexpensive pocket calculators.

6. You can always have some fun with specialty advertising items. This is especially true if you are selling to a high-end creative market such as advertising agencies or entertainment clients. Some examples of these kinds of promotional items include baseball caps, T-shirts, flying saucers, fortune cookies, customized candy jars, travel accessories including toothbrushes and first aid kits, yo-yos, and balloons.

Specialty Advertising Premium Items

1. Clients that reach a certain level of sales or respond to a special offer can be rewarded with more expen-

sive specialty advertising items. One of the most popular for office use is the customized clock or watch.

2. More expensive clothing items are another example of premium specialty advertising. Polo shirts and baseball jackets are two of the most popular choices.

3. Another idea is to use high-quality attaché or briefcases, sports bags and tote bags.

4. Expensive office electronics, such as high-quality calculators and desktop or personal radios, also make good specialty advertising premium gifts.

5. High-quality office items can also be customized. Examples include pen and pencil sets, desk pad sets, leather notepad holders and personal organizers.

6. The ultimate specialty advertising premium is the award item. These are for specific and limited situations, such as for clients that have been with you for a very long time or clients that purchase a large volume of services within a specific time frame. Examples of these very special and distinctive awards include crystal paperweights, unique plaques or even your own specially designed trophy.

Marketing & Promoting Your Work

SUPER STRATEGY

THREE

Don't Overlook the Value of a Business Card

"I hand out lots of business cards. You can follow the development of my company through the changes in my business cards. Aside from designing a logo, I didn't give much thought to self-promotion other than creating a business card. I had my core list of clients and for the first eighteen months, work came in pretty steadily. By the end of 1989, work slowed, and I realized it was because I had done no promoting since I started. I have found that it takes about three to six months for a prospect to turn into a project, so if I want to have work in six months, I had better do something today.

"Most of the promotion I do is through referrals. I spend a lot of time on the phone. I go out and see people. I decided my business card would have to do more than tell people where to send the check.

"With my second business card I got businesslike. I went about promoting myself as the following: a design *company* that specialized in desktop publishing/digital design. I changed the name of the company to Michael Pilla & Associates with the idea of appearing more like a business than an independent designer and I promoted my

expertise with the Mac.

"My business card was designed to reflect this: the gray and maroon colors, the small understated logo, the two-line description of what I do.

"Unfortunately, the results were not as I expected. In a sense it worked too well. I had hoped that the desktop work would lead to some design jobs, that the DTP stuff would be an entrée to larger stuff. I have done desktop jobs for MTV and Colgate Pal-

SUPER STRATEGY

THREE

continued from page 17

molive, but, like my other DTP clients, I have had no luck in turning them into design clients. They saw me as providing a specific service, and I am sure my business-like demeanor added to the perception. Maybe I did too good a job at something I wasn't really interested in. In any event, I was not perceived as a creative person, but as a teckie. The card was too specific!

"For my third card, I went back to basics, not happy with the quality of work I had been getting. It seems clients go the desktop route when they don't want to pay for a designer. I went back to my beginnings to see what worked well for me originally. I went back and analyzed my roots.

"From the beginning I had decided to function as a small independent studio. I would not work for another studio or agency. I would not do mechanicals or pure production work and would seldom work for an hourly rate. I was selling my personality.

"I had deviated from this premise, and it cost me. So much for being sensible! I stopped talking about the computer. Basically, I am an artist. I changed the name of my company back to Michael Pilla Design. I removed any pretext of being a multiperson company. I made no mention of the services I provide. I stopped acting like a businessman, and went back to being a creative professional. My clients like the idea of dealing with a creative person.

"My new business cards are meant to be a unique and personal expression, and vague enough to cover any contingency. I put together a simple line version of the card as an interim. Even this simple version caused a dramatic difference in how people saw me and the work I got. The results were even better when I had the color card and a whole 'ID Kit' printed.

"I only get referrals now. No one calls me with computer questions anymore. My billings have gone up substantially, as has the complexity of the projects."

Michael Pilla
Michael Pilla Design

Michael Pilla Design

37 West 26th Street
10th Floor
New York, NY 10010
Tel. 212-686-6567
Fax 212-545-0218

Michael Pilla Design

37 West 26th Street
10th Floor
New York, NY 10010
Tel. 212-686-6567
Fax 212-545-0218

Chapter One Checklist
Yes! You Can Do It All!

Target Your Markets

☐ Decide if you want to do more of the same work or a different kind of work.

☐ And, use the targeting techniques described on pages 6-7 to determine if you want to market yourself by:
- style
- industry
- usage

Find the Time to Do It

☐ Take a business-first attitude.
You are a businessperson first, then a designer.

☐ Plan for success.
The key to successful goal achievement is to write it down.

☐ Stay motivated.
Complete the self-diagnostic test on page 11 to determine if you:
- lack confidence
- are afraid
- feel alone and adrift
- all of the above.

☐ Manage stress; don't let it manage you.
- Accept that you'll never get everything done.
- Accept that you'll never make everybody happy.
- Learn how to say "no."

☐ Find more time.
Everyone wastes time. The successful businessperson identifies how this is happening, eliminates the low-priority activities and uses this new-found time for more important tasks.

☐ Use your time more wisely, by:
- Transferring every item from your marketing plan onto your calendar.
- Not being distracted from completing priority tasks.
- Preparing in advance for meetings by organizing all pertinent information as soon as you schedule a meeting.

Chapter Two
Getting the Word Out

STEP ONE

Make use
of direct mail.

●

STEP TWO

Advertise your services.

●

STEP THREE

Toot your own horn.

●

STEP FOUR

Network when possible.

Now that you have identified your target markets, you need a structured plan for indirect or non-personal promotion. Indirect promotion uses three main tools: direct mail, advertising and publicity. This chapter shows with examples and a case study how these tools can help you build a successful promotional plan.

Be sure to plan a budget for your overall promotional effort. Good accounting standards call for an average of 10 percent of projected gross income to be set aside each year for marketing. Use projected income—what you want to make—rather than last year's income. This way you will be marketing for the future, not the past! So, for example, if you plan to make $100,000, you'll spend an average of $10,000 to do it.

STEP 1 Make Use of Direct Mail

First, what is direct mail? Many designers assume it means mailing promotional material and then making a call to see if the client received the piece. No! The entire concept of direct mail marketing turns on the fact that you have designed a campaign of promotional materials with a specific objective, usually to have clients call you for more information on your services. Then you sell to them once they have called. If you mail, and then call, that is a sales or telemarketing campaign (see chapter three).

Twelve Tips for Creating a Successful Direct Mail Campaign

1. Design to your highest level of technical and creative ability. Make the marketing pieces as compelling as your best client projects.

2. Design for the new industry you are targeting, not the industry you are securely entrenched in. If all of your current clients are in health care and your goal is to attract entertainment clients, a direct mail piece designed for the latter won't make a lot of sense to your existing clients. If your current clients are so different from the clients you want to get work from, don't send current clients the mailing.

3. Remember your marketing goal. Did you decide to focus on selling style, industry specialization or us-

age? Clients in a particular industry will need promotional materials that show your ability to solve their problems. On the other hand, clients that buy style are not industry specific. You can show these clients examples of your style from any industrial application. Finally, if you are selling your skills for newsletter or brochure usage, design your marketing materials to showcase this specialization.

4. Look for materials that can be used in more than one marketing plan. For example, an annual report for a health care company can be used as a "case study" for a direct mail campaign for either an annual report (usage) or health care (industry specific) marketing goal.

5. Add credibility as often as possible to your direct mail marketing materials. This can be in the form of client testimonials, case studies of actual jobs, or mention of membership in professional associations or awards. Credentials are more important to clients buying design skills that are industry specific or usage related. Clients who buy style tend to be bigger risk-takers, therefore credibility is less critical.

6. Plan spaced repetition of your mailings. There really isn't any hard-and-fast rule, except mailings should be geared to the clients' volume of jobs. For example, advertising agen-

cies have a very fast turnover of jobs and you can mail to them more frequently—say every six to eight weeks. If you are marketing to architects, you'll probably only need quarterly mailings because they work at a slower pace. If your mailings are too close together, you'll lose effectiveness; if they're too far apart, you won't build recognition.

7. Once you have designed your direct mail campaign, stick to your schedule for production, printing and mailing. You could have the greatest concept and design, but if the pieces don't get mailed on schedule, you won't be successful!

8. When designing your materials, plan how you might reuse them for future mailings. For example, design a promotional calendar so that when it goes out of date you can cut the dates off and use the remainder as a flyer.

9. Decide before you design your direct mail what you want your client (or prospective client) to do when they get the mailing. Set a specific goal—do you want them to call? Be impressed? Anticipate the next mailing? Refer you to their friends? If you are not clear on your expectations, your clients won't be able to figure it out!

10. Sometimes you can increase client inquiries by making an offer that

they will find of value. In return for their response, perhaps you can offer a poster, a "how-to" guide, a calendar—something of value that promotes you.

11. When you are including copy in your direct mail, be sure it is written from the client's perspective. For example, it is more effective to write, "You need a packaging designer that can help you sell your products," rather than, "I am a great packaging designer."

12. Direct mail response seems to be greater when the personality of the designer is strongly reflected. Clients are people, too! Direct mail by its nature is a very impersonal promotional tool, so try to put yourself into the mailing. You can add a portrait, biographical information, or make a statement of your personal philosophy. Anything that says, "This is the person you'll be working with."

Direct Mail Dos and Don'ts Checklist

☐ Do address your mail to a person. People buy design, companies or job titles don't.

☐ Do have a detailed profile of your targeted client in mind when developing your campaign.

☐ Do offer clear goal-oriented instructions for the client—what do you want them to do?

☐ Don't worry about your mail being tossed aside. Speak to the percentage of people who will respond, not the ones who won't.

☐ Don't plan just direct mail pieces, plan campaigns.

☐ Do make it very easy to respond—use large type for phone numbers, include business reply cards, an 800 phone number—plan ahead!

☐ Do give a deadline for response whenever appropriate. It will keep your mailer from being placed in a pile of papers and lost.

☐ Don't just create passive "look at me" mail. Try interactive mailing where the client participates in some way, for example, a die-cut printed piece the client can put together.

☐ Do consider designing a "keeper," that is, a promotional piece that has some function or use such as a calendar or notepad.

☐ Don't start direct mail promotion without planning a budget and timeline for production.

SUPER STRATEGY

FOUR

Establish Recognition and Presence

"This promo piece is a direct result of four experienced designers going into a new partnership in 1987. Because of the unusual coincidence of the alphabetical order of the names of the principals, we were able to design a piece to establish instant recognition and presence.

"The Alphabet Soup promo was first printed in 1987, redone and reprinted in 1992, and is currently being revised in 1994. With the combination of great graphics and interesting copy, it is a piece that always gets remembered and gets a reaction. In addition, the concept Alphabet Soup plays off of the full range of design services printed in the upper right corner of each page.

"Though the piece is expensive, $25 to $30 per piece, we have found it much less expensive than a $200 to $300 sales call by one of our principals to generate work. We have had Fortune 500 companies that received the piece two to three years ago pass it around within the corporation, so we get a pass-along readership unlike normal design promotions. One very important factor to keep the piece updated is that ongoing projects are photographed as they are completed. Then, when we want to update the piece, it is less work."

Drew Haygeman

HIJK

STEP 2 Advertise Your Services

Like direct mail, the objective in advertising your design services usually is not to sell, but to stimulate some kind of response. In responding, the prospective client becomes qualified for the process of selling. You also can do image advertising, where the objective is to reinforce recognition, but only when that is an appropriate objective in your strategy.

Display Advertising

Assuming response is the objective, you must design your display with two objectives: (1) express your marketing goal (to get packaging design work); and (2) ask for a response.

Different marketing messages will need different ad campaigns. It is very important that you start with a client profile. Know who your client is. What do they read? Where should you place your ad so they will see it? Don't overlook small circulation publications such as association newsletters. Once you have a list of all the publications your targeted clients read, call and get media kits to determine and compare publication rates. You don't have to do full-page ads in four color. A quarter-page black-and-white ad in a local business magazine may be more effective!

Free Listings

Advertising does not have to cost money. There are annual directories that offer free (or very low-cost) copy-only ads that work as a directory of designers for clients to choose from. Most list just the firm name, address, phone and fax number. However, when you have the opportunity to add a "specialty" line, be sure to use all the available characters (anywhere from twenty to one hundred) to spell out your marketing message. Here is a partial list of annual directories to contact for your free listing.

The Workbook, 940 N. Highland, Los Angeles, CA 90038

The Design Directory, P.O. Box 1591, Evanston, IL 60204

New Media, 915 Broadway, New York, NY 10010

Corporate Showcase, 915 Broadway, New York, NY 10010

Black Book Media Group, 115 5th Avenue, New York, NY 10003

Southwest Portfolio 7041 E. Orange Blossom Lane, Scottsdale, AZ 85253

Advertise Your Services

Ad Design Checklist

☐ Use one marketing message per advertisement. This is not the medium for telling prospective clients everything you do, just the work you want to do more of.

☐ Say what makes you special? It could be some kind of expertise, equipment, the location of your studio, the number of languages you speak. Don't be just another designer that does logos; let prospective clients know what makes your logo work so special.

☐ As in your direct mail, add a note of credibility. All clients can tell from your ad is that you could afford the ad! Use client quotes or mention association membership to build believability.

☐ Plan campaigns, not just ads. You're in this for the long run.

☐ Show your most extraordinary work, not necessarily work you have done for a client. Don't be afraid to use self-assignments in your advertising.

☐ Plan a minimum number of exposures to build recognition. For example, if the display ad is in an annual directory, plan on at least three consecutive years of advertising. If the publication is monthly, plan at least six to eight insertions out of twelve.

SUPER STRATEGY

FIVE

Advertise in the Yellow Pages

"We have been advertising in the Business to Business Yellow Pages and have been very successful. We run two completely different ads. The first under packaging is a smaller ad. It is really just an enlarged listing advertising us as specialists in packaging design.

"Our second ad is under graphic design and is a larger display ad, shown here. Since we advertise ourselves as generalists in design, our logo and minimalist design speak to our specific style. This ad then attracts the kind of client interested in our style and is a client we're more likely to want to work with. For an ad like this to work, you have to show your design viewpoint or style, not just what you do as a designer."

Patty Wong
Patty Wong Design

PATRICIA WONG & ASSOCIATES

Logos/Trademarks • Brochures
Corporate Identity • Annual
Reports • Packaging • Displays

2091 Business Center Dr. Suite 215
Irvine, California 92715

(714) 476-1213

SUPER STRATEGY

SIX

Combine Diversity and Consistency

"I have always found that a diversity of promotional material consistent in style is the most successful. Not only does it keep me from getting bored with self-promotion, but I find it more cost-effective.

"I print a black-and-white postcard, which is a sample of my design and illustration, to use informally. When I am not selling to clients and am just corresponding with them, they receive a subtle sales message.

"I print promotional postcards from assignment work. I mail these quarterly as I am certain I will have enough interesting work to select from at this point.

"I use holiday cards created on a co-op

basis with four or five people, but do find it very difficult to coordinate and organize when more people are involved.

"When negotiating an assignment, I make sure to include the printing of an overrun for promotional material. I usually plan at least a 1,000 print run.

"My most successful promo piece has been my miniportfolio. I can use leftover postcards from my quarterly mailing, design a cover, add a plastic comb binding, and it's finished. The reason this has been so successful is that it is a unique promo the client gets to keep, and they also see a 'grocery list' of my services. The first ten that I mailed brought me $8,000 in billings."

Darlene McElroy
Darlene McElroy Design/Illustration

STEP 3 Toot Your Own Horn

Getting publicity through winning design competitions or being featured in your local paper is probably the most overlooked area of self-promotion. Like direct mail and advertising, the goal of publicity is not to sell; it's to get attention.

On the plus side, publicity carries tremendous credibility, which you can also transfer to your marketing campaign. The downside is, there are no guarantees that it will be published.

Here are two avenues for publicity and credibility.

1. Enter competitions

Research all the client (trade) and design industry publications that hold annual "creative" awards. You get the immediate exposure upon entering when, quite often, your potential clients are the jurors. If you win, you get publication exposure. Then, you get to write your own media release, further expanding on the equity you are earning from the (usually quite modest) entry fee.

2. Get published

Submit your work to book publishers for consideration in their annual design compendiums. North Light Books, for example, publishes a book in the Fresh Ideas series twice a year; swapfiles like these often include addresses of included designers in the back of the book—enabling anyone who likes your work to contact you. Contact design magazines about having your work featured. They are always looking to "discover" new talent. Again, acceptance is newsworthy enough for you to generate a media release.

Develop a Media Database

Distribute media releases when you do something newsworthy. Identify the media you will submit releases to and build a media database for a mailing list. Unlike placing advertising, when you buy space only where prospective clients can see your ad, submit your publicity as widely and broadly as possible to magazines, newspapers and newsletters read by both present and prospective clients, other designers and your community.

Follow the Right Format

Use a standard media release format to submit your news to the media. Editors receive hundreds of press releases a week, so be sure you conform to the standard format to avoid having your release thrown away! The release should begin at least one-third of the way down the page; it should be double-spaced with wide margins; and it should conclude with a "-30-" or "###." Enclose samples or photos whenever possible to increase the media interest and your chances of being published. Be sure to print the release on letterhead; it looks more professional than a photocopy of the letterhead. Here are some sample press releases—note the rigidly designed format and don't forget to double space!

SUPER STRATEGY

SEVEN

A First Effort That Worked

"We had just opened our doors the summer of 1992 when this piece was created. Since we had no clients and no salespeople, our first marketing effort was to create a direct mail piece that would encourage potential clients to try our studio. We needed to communicate our capabilities visually, as well as with copy, and chose the rabileon (half rabbit, half chameleon) as our mascot. We spent $3,000 to print 3,000 pieces. We mailed 1,000 out as an invitation, and held 2,000 for later leave-behind pieces. We mailed the first group out in the fall of 1992 through November of 1992. The mailing resulted in $75,000 in billing.

"Copy and design specifications were as follows: (1) This was to be an invitation to a private session on the Shima equipment with a two-hour time limit. (2) They will have the opportunity to learn how this technology has revolutionized the world of digital imaging and image compositing. (3) Ask them to bring something that they are working on and we will show them how it works

Reality isn't what it used to be.

on the system. (4) They can call to arrange an appointment to come to the studio at their convenience any time between 8 A.M. and 8 P.M. (5) We will provide food. (6) This is an exclusive invitation; however, we encourage them to bring another print production manager or art director with them. (7) There is a one-month time limit to take advantage of this offer."

Judy Linden
Metafor Imaging

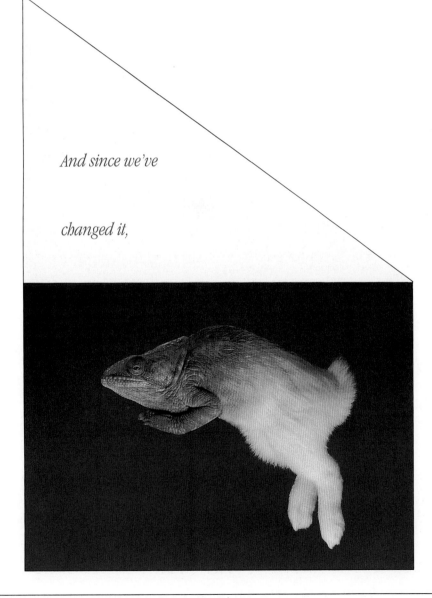

And since we've

changed it,

SUPER STRATEGY

EIGHT

How Indirect Marketing Works

"Direct contact with clients is not the only way to get work. I have been generating job leads from indirect sources, such as publications and manufacturers.

"For example, a submission to Step-By-Step Graphics Electronic Design newsletter resulted in a cover story and interview with samples of my work. As a result two companies from Japan called for computer textbook projects and I got a new clip art client.

"*Magazine Printing Journal* called from my Source Book ad for a submission of my

Darlene McElroy created "Computer PMS" in Aldus Freehand to use on a self-promotional mailer.

Ever have one of those days?

NEWPORT BEACH, Calif.—Darlene McElroy markets her work as "saucy computer illustration that's created in Aldus Freehand by a playful mind." McElroy is one of the new breed of artists that take advantage of the tools of desktop publishing to create compelling digital art. Proving that the sophistication of the system does not determine the quality of the final product, she works on a Macintosh IIci with 36mb of RAM/80 internal hard drive with an extra gigabyte external drive. A 20-T Supermatch color monitor and a Microtek 600zs ScanMaker make up the rest of her desktop system, while black and white proofing is done on a HP Laserjet 4M. Digital art is easy to use and easy to transport—this picture fit on a floppy with room to spare since the four-color, EPS-version file size was only 334k. It doesn't take much in terms of hardware, but artistic talent must come first.

Sir Speedy, Kodak plan joint Photo CD launch

SAN FRANCISCO Sir Speedy, Inc., the nation's largest business printer, joined Eastman Kodak Company in announcing a unique agreement involving the launch of Kodak's Photo CD Portfolio format.

Sir Speedy released a list of 320 locations in 37 states plus Mexico that are now ready to produce Kodak Portfolio CD discs for customers. The joint announcement was made January 5 at MacWorld Expo '94.

"We're proud to be first with widespread capability to produce Portfolio CD discs for our customers," said Don Lowe, president of the Laguna Hills, Calif.-based franchiser. "

For a long time, Sir Speedy has been on the leading edge of business-printing technology, including breakthroughs such as high-speed copying, computer graphics, fax services, short-run color printing and color copying. We see the CD as a communications tool for the turn of the century.

"We are positioning ourselves as being not only in the printing business, but in the business of information distribution. CD technology will provide us another vehicle for distributing that information. It's a natural extension of our current business."

One CD can hold the equivalent of 100 color photographs, 500 floppy disks or 250,000 pieces of paper, according to Lowe.

Kodak's new Portfolio CD will allow Sir Speedy and their electronic imaging subsidiary, Copies Now, franchisees to create affordable multi-media presentations of photos, graphics, text and sound for customers, who can then play the discs on a computer, a television set or a CD-I player.

To create a Portfolio CD presentation, customers will assemble all of the required images, graphics and sound, and bring them a participating location.

If necessary Sir Speedy or Copies Now can do the creative work for customers. Images can be provided on film, computer media or on Photo CD disc.

Customers can also have their

See page 13 ➤

work. As a result of that story, I was asked to demonstrate the software I had used at trade shows for the manufacturer. Great promotion and visibility.

"Hot on the trail of the software manufacturers, I sent the Capri Son piece out of my portfolio to Aldus Corporation. As a result, they purchased a limited use as a cover and I traded 500 printed copies and free software for part of the fee.

"Finally, I always enter competitions held by the sourcebooks for the design and illustration of their divider tab pages. These are very competitive, but offer great exposure when you are accepted, as I was."

Darlene McElroy
Darlene McElroy Design/Illustration

Getting the word out about you and your new marketing message should also be done by the traditional "word of mouth" method. Whether you choose ad and direct mail campaigns or not, networking should be part of your marketing strategy. Joining associations will not only bring you to the attention of prospective clients, it will also provide opportunities to buy mailing lists, advertise to a pre-qualified audience, publicize your business in association newsletters, and participate in public service projects. Your peer association membership is also important to your self-promotion plan. Other designers offer professional support, inside industry information and referrals. In addition, you can use the membership as a professional credential in your advertising and direct mail promotions!

When to Send Out a Media Release

A newsworthy item to submit to the media can be generated at anytime! Here is a list of business activities that is possible media release fodder. Have you:

- recently opened or moved your business?

- added full- or part-time staff?

- added or expanded your services?

- been in a juried show or exhibit?

- won a competition?

- completed an interesting or unusual client project?

- written a book?

- been involved in public service or pro bono projects?

- conducted seminars or lectures?

- been elected to an association board or committee?

MARIA PISCOPO
2038 CALVERT
COSTA MESA, CA
92626-3520
(714) 556-8133
fax
(714) 556-0899

FOR IMMEDIATE RELEASE
Add today's date here

FOR INFORMATION CONTACT:
Maria Piscopo
(714) 556-8133

CREATIVE SERVICES ADDS NEW SERVICE

Costa Mesa.....Maria Piscopo, owner of Creative Services, has just returned from the Apple Computer training center in San Francisco and announced her firm's added services of computer-based retouching and illustration services. Piscopo comments, "My clients need us to provide more assistance to them and take on more of the responsibility for image production. We're <u>not just</u> a design firm anymore."

The expansion includes advanced computer and digital printing equipment and high-resolution image-enhancement software. Piscopo feels this added capability is essential to business, "Clients <u>don't</u> think in terms of needing computer imaging, as much as they want visual solutions that are fast and cost-effective."

Piscopo has been an illustrator and designer based in Costa Mesa, California, for ten years and is a current member of the American Institute of Graphic Arts.

###

MARIA PISCOPO
2038 CALVERT
COSTA MESA, CA
92626-3520
(714) 556-8133
fax
(714) 556-0899

FOR IMMEDIATE RELEASE
Add today's date here

FOR INFORMATION CONTACT:
Maria Piscopo
(714) 556-8133

AREA ILLUSTRATOR RELOCATES STUDIO

Costa Mesa.....Designer/illustrator Maria Piscopo has relocated her studio to Calvert Street, Costa Mesa, California. Piscopo has just returned from a sixteen-month world tour including the countries of Java, Thailand, Morocco and Greece. In her travels, she met and worked with other artists in France and Italy.

As an illustrator and designer, her clients have included: AVCO Finance, Carnation, Kawasaki and Carl's Jr. Her work has been honored by the Society of Illustrators, the Public Relations Society of America and the Orange County Ad Club.

Her work with art students has brought her teaching positions at Golden West and Orange Coast Community Colleges. Piscopo feels her new "international" point of view will benefit both clients and students in the future.

###

Chapter Two Checklist:
Getting the Word Out

STEP 1 — Make Use of Direct Mail

To get off on the right foot in the design and use of your direct mail materials, consider these twelve guidelines.

☐ Design your direct mail pieces to the highest level of technical and creative ability that you can.

☐ Design for the new industry you are targeting, not the industry in which you are securely entrenched, if these industries are dissimilar.

☐ Remember your marketing goal and design your pieces so they support your goal.

☐ Look among your design samples for pieces that can be used in more than one marketing plan.

☐ Add credibility as often as possible to your direct mail materials, in the form of client testimonials, project case studies, and mention of awards or professional memberships.

☐ Plan spaced repetition of your mailings.

☐ Once you have designed your campaign, stick to your schedule for production, printing and mailing.

☐ When designing, plan ahead for how you might reuse marketing materials in a different way for future mailings.

☐ Make sure your pieces tell the prospective client what it is you want him to do: Call, return an attached postcard, wait for the next mailing, what?

☐ Increase inquiries by offering a calendar, notepad, poster, etc., in return for a response.

☐ Always, always, always consider the client's point of view. Ask yourself this question: Why should they hire you? Then, use your marketing materials to answer it.

☐ Always, always, always reflect your personality in your pieces. After all, you are human!

STEP 2 — Advertise Your Services

☐ Use display advertising in newspapers, magazines, trade journals, etc., to:
  • express your marketing goal
  • ask potential clients to respond.

☐ Remember these golden rules of designing ads:
  • Use one message per ad.
  • Make sure it's clear what makes you special.
  • As in direct mail, add credibility whenever possible.
  • Plan campaigns, not just ads.
  • Be discriminating. Show only your extraordinary work.
  • Plan a minimum number of publication or directory exposures to build recognition.

Toot Your Own Horn

☐ Get publicity and increase your credibility by:
- entering design competitions.
- getting written up in your local press.

☐ Develop a media database for use when you distribute releases about your newsworthy accomplishments.

☐ Send out media releases when you have:
- recently opened or moved your business.
- added full- or part-time staff.
- added or expanded your services.
- been in a juried show or exhibit.
- won a competition.
- completed a particularly interesting project.
- written a book.
- been involved in a public service or pro bono project.
- conducted seminars or lectures.
- been elected to an association board or committee.

☐ Remember to use the standard media release format described on page 29.

Network When Possible

☐ Join associations.

☐ Participate in public service projects.

Chapter Three
Making Contact

STEP ONE

Set up a database.

STEP TWO

Research new clients.

STEP THREE

Identify the contact
person.

STEP FOUR

Make the appointment.

STEP FIVE

Present your portfolio.

Now that the word is out with your advertising, direct mail and public relations campaign, you can begin the personal promotion phase and make direct contact with potential clients. As opposed to "cold calling," where there is no recognition factor, this is "warm calling"!

Non-personal promotion tools such as ads, mailings and publicity create valuable equity in your self-promotion strategy. Like real estate, this equity is the increase in value of your self-promotion program based on what you paid for it and what it is worth when you call someone who has seen it.

STEP 1 Set Up a Database

The old days of the shoebox and index cards for keeping track of information on clients and prospective clients are long gone. Today, a computer database is required for maximum effectiveness and efficiency in your search for new business. There are many different software programs available for databases; both for MAC and PC systems. Selecting the best one for you is not always as easy as getting a word-of-mouth referral or buying what's on sale this week at the local software warehouse. You may want to hire a consultant to give a demonstration and make recommendations. Many designers use the database in their existing project management programs, such as FileMaker/Pro, to manage client data. Some word processing programs such as Professional File and Write, come with their own database programs.

There are two basic directions you can go when shopping for the right program. You can buy a program that has a preexisting client profile form and fields of information. This is great if this is your first database, because you simply input the client profile information from your index cards into the existing fields. (A field of information is anything you want to retrieve later, such as addresses, phone numbers or dates of client contacts.) You spend less time at the front end in the setup, but generally have less flexibility. Or you can buy a program that requires you to design the client profile form (also called "record") and specify both the fields and layout of the form. You spend more time at the front end in the start-up, but it will be exactly what you want.

Either way, with any typical database format, your client profile will look something like the following example. A colon following a word creates a "field" and allows that information to be searched for and retrieved at a later time.

alpha: (allows alphabetical retrieval for firm names like John Smith & Company; at this field you would type "smith")

firm:

address:

city:

state:

zip:

contact:

first name:

(The above allows for printing mailing labels or merging with a word processing program for personal letters. Keep in mind, the postal service prefers the last line of a mailing label be the zip code, not the name of your contact!

addl: (usually additional contact name, such as a secretary)

phone:

fax:

date last: (date of last contact)

type: (type of contact—phone call? appointment?)

date next: (date for next contact)

Here are optional, but very useful, fields for managing the information in your database:

type client: (manufacturer? ad agency? magazine?)

product: (usually a code, such as "f" for food clients)

project name: (for follow-up and estimating purposes)

remarks: (where lead came from, or any other comments)

status: (usually a code to distinguish current vs. prospective clients)

Designing the form for the "client profile" is critically important for future follow-up. For example, the profile allows the following scenarios: When you make appointments, you can call prospective clients sorted by zip code, so you're not driving back and forth from one end of town to the other. You can call all current clients you talked to in January that said to call back in March. You can mail new promo pieces to all prospective clients that you showed your food packaging portfolio to last month. You can mail a different promo piece to magazines and corporations. All from one form!

Marketing & Promoting Your Work

SUPER STRATEGY

A Strategy for Making Contact

"The first thing that we do is develop leads from sourcebooks such as *Artist's & Graphic Designer's Market* and *Children's Writer's & Illustrator's Market*. Both are Writer's Digest Books publications. Then we plant the seeds for getting an appointment with a direct mail campaign of postcards. For getting the appointment, we generally have to make a phone call, mail a promo, and then call back for the appointment. The time line for this process usually takes from three to nine months. Next, we have a core portfolio representing our style and build around it with specific pieces for this client and new work we want to show. We have found that trying to second-guess what the client wants to see doesn't work. This has given us the confidence to put in work we love. I have to ignore the impulse I have to throw everything out I think might scare the client and throw everything in to cover all the bases. There is no such thing as a perfect portfolio. We go for showing our best work and look for a good fit with the client.

"Finally, for promotional material, we use a die sublimation printer that allows us

'weird dog' digital medium

LeVan/Barbee

A A

30 Ipswich Street Studio 211
Boston Massachusetts 02215
telephone/fax 617 536 6828

Phone for Illustration Portifolio: Print or Disk

to change images at will and do one or a zillion. We also like the image quality a whole lot more than either laser prints or iris prints, not to mention the control and instant gratification the printer gives us."

Susan LeVan
LeVan/Barbee

The more you know about prospective clients, the better presentations you make. The better the presentation, the more likely you'll find work. Doing your homework requires the establishment of a marketing goal so you'll know where to start looking for new clients. Here are seven major sources for finding prospective clients.

Daily Newspaper

The daily newspaper business section always has information on new products, services, expansions and personnel changes that give you the opportunity to get your foot in the door. For example, a news item that is headlined, "ABC Food Company Launches Six New Products" can be translated into a lead for food packaging design.

Office Park Directories

Office or industrial park directories give you the names and types of tenants. All of these may not be the kind of clients you ultimately want to work with, but they make a great "bread and butter" client base from which to launch a self-promotion strategy. Your presentation will be based on being their "local" design firm, conveniently available for their needs and services.

Magazines

Editorial calendars of magazines you want to work with list the theme for each issue. This information is very valuable when approaching the publication for work. Instead of being just another designer that wants to show a portfolio, you can discuss how you can meet the magazines' needs and concerns.

Trade Shows

Trade shows in any industry-specific marketing strategy are one of the best sources for new business. Not every company exhibits in their own industry trade show, but the ones that do are always going to need more promotional materials, design and printing services than the ones that stay home!

Design Annuals

Design annuals are a good place to look for clients that have a strong sense of style and are willing to take creative risks. These "best of the best" annual awards programs recognize firms that take chances and don't always play it "safe." You can bet that if a firm used highly creative and stylish design once, they would probably do it again.

Business Directories

The bulk of your database of prospective clients will actually come from annual directories available in your local library reference section. Many of these directories are now available on disk and make the entire process of setting up a file much easier—no keyboard work required! See the Library Reference Directories sidebar for the books.

Library Reference Directories

- Advertising Agencies: *Standard Directory of Advertising Agencies*; *ADWEEK Agency Directory*

- Client Direct (Corporate Clients): *Standard Directory of Advertisers*; *Chamber of Commerce Directory*; *State Services Directory* (e.g. *California Services Directory*); *State Manufacturers Register* (e.g. *Massachusetts Manufacturers Register*); *Business Journal Incorporated Book of Lists* (available on disk); *Encyclopedia of Associations* (by industry)

- Direct Marketing Agencies: *Directory of Major Mailers*; *Direct Marketing Market Place*

- Magazines and Editorial Clients: *Standard Rate & Data Service*; *Gebbie Press All-In-One Directory*; *Gale Directory of Publications & Broadcast Media*; *Editor & Publisher*—newspaper directory

- Other Design Firms: *Design Firm Directory for Graphic & Industrial Design* (Wefler & Assoc.); *The Workbook* (Directory Section)

- Paper Products/Book Publishers/Record Album Producers: *Artist's Market*

- Representatives/Galleries/Fine Art Reps: *A Guide To Literary Agents & Art/Photo Reps*

- Databases: *Gale Directory of Databases*

Identify Contact Person

Once you have the basic information on the firm you want to work with, the next step is to identify the true client, the individual with the responsibility and authority to hire you. The best way to approach this step is to write a "script" for the phone call you are about to make. Scripts are simply preparation for an interaction with a client or potential client where you have set a specific objective and must accomplish it with confidence and efficiency. In this step, the objective is to get the name of the individual who purchases design services.

Here's a typical script:

"Hello, this is (your name) from (your firm) and I'm updating the information we have on your company. Who is the person in charge of (the work you want to do for them)?"

Getting the name, and the person's job title, is all you need to do!

SUPER STRATEGY

TEN

Develop a Sense of Teamwork

"We bring a certain array of skills and expertise to projects. We are in step and have a sense of teamwork. We develop our clients' ideas. We work hard to establish trust. It takes a certain type of client to like working that way. But our promo piece is attracting that type of client. We believe in a lot of information exchange up front. Everything possible is spelled out in the beginning. We don't like surprises!"

Donham keeps clients coming back because

"We put a lot of energy into doing the projects right. We try to fit our clients' needs. We try to stay lean and billable. Part of it is the level of design we give for the price. We believe that money is real, so our clients get their money's worth. Responsibility in pricing is a good investment."

Lynn Donham
Church Street Design

STEP 4 Make the Appointment

Because you have done your homework and matched yourself and your marketing goal with the client that needs the work you want to do, you can take an "assumptive" approach to getting an appointment to present your portfolio. You can presume that, if your call is properly scripted, the prospective client can decide whether to meet with you based on their need at the time you call.

A sample script:

"Hello, this is (your name) from (your firm) and I'm calling regarding providing your firm with (your services). When would be a good time for us to meet?"

This typical script prompts the prospective client to decide (a) there is a need and he will meet with you, or (b) there is no need and he doesn't need to meet with you. When you approach a client this way, he can make an informed and efficient choice! If he decides not to meet with you, your script then calls for you to ask, "When should I check back with you?"

SUPER STRATEGY
E·L·E·V·E·N

Evaluate Your Client's Needs

"We used to approach clients on a project basis. Now we approach clients by evaluating their need for projects. We also get to know the middle manager and his or her needs and concerns.

"We keep a client database of information on repeat projects, such as catalogs, with the result of locking the client in for the benefit of the convenience to them. We've developed new products, such as in-house multimedia and can do sales presentations on disc or CD.

"Each client builds a relationship with all of our associates. So we hire very carefully. In a job interview, we look for design talent and relationship skills. This takes time now, but saves grief later and helps us build long-term client relationships."

Trina Gardner-Nuovo

White + Associates

Present Your Portfolio

The problem with the term "portfolio presentation" is that it implies a one-way flow of information. To simply present yourself and your work will not result in enough information for you to follow up and will probably waste your client's precious time. The better approach is a *consultation* to discuss their needs and your ability to meet those needs. Since this makes each appointment with a prospective client unique, you can't really script ahead what you will say, but you can prepare in advance. Here are considerations for a "client consultation" with sample scripts:

Prepare an Introduction

Even though you may have made this appointment the day before, the person interviewing you has had many distractions since your call. While you are settling in for your meeting, review how you arrived at their door. Was it a referral? a listing in a directory? an item in the newspaper? State what you will be covering in your meeting as a "reality check" for the prospective client. This is their opportunity to let you know of any changes in their needs and to this meeting's agenda.

Sample script:

"As we discussed yesterday, I saw your firm's product line expansion mentioned in the local paper. We will look over samples from my portfolio that relate to your new products."

Go Behind the Scenes

When you are showing your portfolio, be sure to focus on the "who, how and why" and not just the "what." Your client can clearly see what you are presenting whether it is an annual report, packaging or a newsletter. It is the creative process and problem-solving that went into the work they need to hear about. Discuss who you did the work for, how you solved the client's problem and why you chose that solution. Design clients are hiring you for what you can do for them based on the problems you have already solved for another client!

Sample scripts:

"In this example of a newsletter design, our challenge was to come up with a two-color look on a one-color budget."

"This annual report project almost stopped when the CEO was suddenly hospitalized and we had to work with a new client contact. Since our policy is always to keep a record of our client meetings, she was able to step in without getting behind schedule."

"For this packaging project, our industry experience helped the new product manager get the job done in time for their annual sales meeting in New York."

What Happens Next

Probably the biggest mistake designers make when presenting a portfolio is not connecting the meeting or "consultation" with the follow-up step. The follow-up to this appointment begins now, in the meeting, not after you have left.

The key to being persistent but not a pest is coming to an agreement or conclusion as to what happens next, after the meeting. There are three options you and your client can discuss and agree on before you leave. First, will you meet again right away? Usually this is when your consultation has stimulated the prospect of a job. Second, will you call them regarding follow-up on a specific project or need? Third, will you mail them updated promotion material as it becomes available? Usually this shows the lowest level of client interest. All of these options are decided on within a time frame so that you can update your database for both "type of contact" and "date for next contact." Since there is always a next contact, this strategy for portfolio consultations eliminates rejection completely! All you need to ask is, "What happens next?"

Ultimately, design work comes from follow-up, not passively presenting your work and waiting for the phone to ring. Do your homework, meet with clients that have the work you want to do, then follow up to get the jobs.

Sample scripts:

To make another appointment—

Present Your Portfolio

"When should we get together again?"

"When would you like to see an updated portfolio?"

To make a follow-up call—

"When should I call you?"

"How about a call next month?"

"When should I call back on that upcoming project?"

To send updated samples—

"How do you want to keep in touch?"

"When should I send more information?"

Ask for a Referral

When you have had a successful consultation and have discussed your prospect's upcoming needs, the final step is to ask for a referral. Be sure to ask an "open-ended" question and not a "yes/no" question.

Sample scripts:

Don't ask closed questions! For example, "Do you know anyone who should see my portfolio?" does not allow the client to take the time to think about your question. The better approach is to ask, "Who do you know that should see my portfolio?"

SUPER STRATEGY
TWELVE

Conduct In-Depth Consultations

"We start by getting basic information about the client's priorities and selection process when making the original appointment. I always plan on taking lots of time for the interview because I've heard very negative reports from clients about designers "clock watching." This basic information allows me to start the interview based on the client's concerns instead of my own.

"We then present a general body of work but relate each piece to one of the client's specific concerns. I have found that good speaking skills are very important, and it is helpful to think fast on your feet. If the client expresses concern because they don't see exactly what they need in our portfolio, we will quote them a fee for developing ideas and thumbnail sketches. We leave the interview with specifications for a cost proposal and don't quote price off the top of our heads. When the client is not specific, we leave 'to be determined' in the quote."

Patty Wong
Patty Wong Design

Assembling a

Let's take a look at how to put together the portfolio. First, throw out the idea that there is such a thing as The Portfolio. One portfolio could not possibly meet the needs of every different presentation. Everyone starts with a *body of work* that breaks down into various portfolios.

For example, a designer will have a body of work made up of every assignment or self-assignment they could show. For a presentation to a health care company, the designer will pull out a portfolio from the main body of work that this client will best relate to, such as other health care projects or projects for service companies.

A portfolio could also be geared to a particular subject, such as packaging design, and any projects related to packaging. The objective of pulling out a portfolio from a body of work is to get as close as possible to work that will meet the prospective client's industry or specific need. Any given portfolio will be about ten to fifteen pieces out of a body of work that may number into the tens or hundreds!

Never show everything in the hope the prospective client will find something they like. This is very different from dealing with the current or ongoing client that has seen (and uses) many different types of work. The prospective client must keep a clear focus on what particular thing you could bring in on that first job. So dif-

ferent situations call for different portfolios pulled out of the overall body of work.

Format

Flexibility in format is all-important. A very flexible portfolio format allows for quick and easy changes without reducing the level of quality of the presentation. There are many different portfolio formats, but they can be divided into two basic types: the book or binder and the individual mounted or laminated portfolio. Also, there are three different kinds of portfolios based on different selling situations: the show portfolio, the traveling portfolio, and the drop-off portfolio.

The *show portfolio* is the one each designer, photographer and illustrator carries around and personally presents to prospective clients. Before we get into a discussion of show portfolio format, however, we need to take a look at the show portfolio case. Clients get an immediate (often indelible) image of you at first glance, so your show portfolio case should look like an extension of the image you want to convey, not something that you haphazardly picked up and put together.

Look for a case that has some personal distinction. A custom case manufactured specifically for your work is one of the best choices. You choose size, color and material, along

...er, buy the more expensi... classic leather, not the cheaper vinyl cases. Or, ask to look through their suppliers' catalogs for something just a little different or unique. Also, don't overlook the possible choices luggage store outlets may offer.

Inside your portfolio case, go for quality and professionalism, because a client may assume that if your show portfolio is poorly produced or presented, the work you would do for them will be, too. Worn mats or unmounted presentation pieces *must* be taken care of immediately.

Now, let's discuss format. For maximum flexibility, individual mounted or laminated pieces are the best choice. Whether mounted or laminated, every piece should have the same outside dimensions. Standard mount boards or laminations range in size from $8'' \times 10''$ to $11'' \times 14''$ (or squares $8'' \times 8''$ to $14'' \times 14''$). The portfolio becomes awkward to carry and present if artwork is much larger than this.

This standardization is extremely important because it allows the prospective client to concentrate on the work instead of different size formats, and it impresses them with

Assembling a Portfolio

your neatness and professionalism! Also, you can easily and quickly create a different portfolio to allow for a different client presentation.

Photographers and illustrators can mount or laminate prints or transparencies of their work; designers can do the same. Designers can also show pieces by using the same size board with a plastic pocket glued to it to hold brochures, catalogs, etc. Printed pieces or tearsheets can be mounted to the same size boards.

The *traveling portfolio* is sent when an out-of-town prospective client needs to see a portfolio. This is as full and complete a portfolio as the one you would show in person, and should contain the same samples.

Because the artist is not there to show the work, the binder is the best format choice. It controls the order in which the work is viewed and minimizes the chance of any pieces getting lost. Most art stores have these binder or book portfolios in various sizes and prices. The 9″ × 12″ ringless type is best because it is the neatest, the pages turn more easily, and it is a convenient size to ship.

A *drop-off portfolio* is different from the show portfolio and the traveling portfolio in that it is often used to show a limited amount of work in order to help the prospective client decide whether they want to see the show portfolio. In selecting content for the drop-off portfolio, concen-

trate on one or two projects that will stimulate the client to want to meet with you in person and see your complete portfolio.

The format of the drop-off portfolio is most often the same as the traveling portfolio. In other words, you can use the same size and style binder, it just contains less work.

Editing Your Work

Next let's look at what you show in a portfolio. You have certainly heard that you "get what you show" in your portfolio. So, first, you must look at the work you *want* to get.

What kind of work do you want to do more of? Be specific as to the type (packaging, brochures, annual reports) or the industry (food, fashion, travel, health care). Then, build your portfolios around this work and approach prospective clients that buy that type of design work.

What if you don't have this work to show? What if you are making a transition, looking for different types of assignments, or just starting out? And what about the client who says, "But I want someone who has *experience* with my product?"

Often, the work you *want* to do is not the kind of work you have been getting. Paid jobs may not reflect your best work. Every designer has been forced to do work within budget confines or has been given creative restrictions that have prevented

them from doing their finest work. *Don't show it!*

Never include a piece in your portfolio just because you got paid to do it. Instead, use *self-assignments*. People hire you as a designer because of what you *can* do, not what you *have* done. Pull out pieces from your portfolio that don't meet your highest level of creativity and technical ability. Once that is done (be merciless), you can see more clearly the holes that need to be filled with self-assignments.

If you want to do more annual reports, you need to create self-assignments built around the problems and solutions you would find in an annual report assignment. If you want to do more product packaging assignments, select a product and produce a portfolio project to promote it.

Self-assignments have a "pretend" client and problem—along with your solution. Collect samples and tear sheets of the kind of work you want to do and then create your self-assignments from this "ideas file." For further assistance, check in with your local creative association. Many of them sponsor annual "portfolio reviews" where you can get your portfolio critiqued and evaluated by reps and clients. Not being a sales call, this review can be the most honest source of feedback you can find!

SUPER STRATEGY

THIRTEEN

Create a Vision Sheet

Robert Skrzynski uses a unique tool called the Vision Sheet to set the tone for client relationships. "The Vision Sheet shows the client that Q Industria is interested in the client's input. We want to produce something that comes from their ideas. It becomes apparent to the client that this is a vehicle for helping both of us arrive at the same destination. Job communication becomes clearer and time spent in trial and error is eliminated.

"When the client reads through the questions on the Vision Sheet, they discover that by answering the questions they are putting down a detailed, well thought-out statement of both their picture of the finished product and its desired purpose. The Vision Sheet asks the client who will see this product, where they will see it, and in which form it will be presented to their market. It also helps the client become familiar with advertising that works or advertising the client wishes to stay away from. This can be very helpful in eliminating wasted time on trial and error as well as defining the position they want to take in their market.

Hello, you are now in possession of this document because you are embarking on a **creative venture**. You are about to put that venture into someone else's hands...ours. You may already have in your head **exactly what you want** from this project, what it will "say", and what it will look like. We need your help to gain that knowledge and provide you with a **perfect finished project**. That is why we furnish this, our **Vision sheet**. This is where you open up your creative mind and we share a look at your vision. We will "see" **your vision** of what you want this project to accomplish as well as what you view as pitfalls and ways to avoid them. Answering the following questions will **help us** make the picture of your successful project **sharp and clear**. The information you will provide will also assist in keeping us **focused** on the same goal. The result is a project that serves the purpose for which it was originally intended **and more**.

continued from page 49

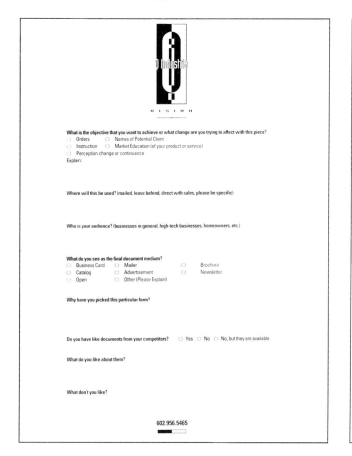

"When the client completes the Vision Sheet, their brain has been picked. They have been required to put down on paper the pictures they have in their mind. They can be more confident that the end result serves the purpose for which it was originally intended. It also eliminates time wasted on efforts in which the client is eventually dissatisfied."

Robert Skrzynski

Q Industria

Chapter Three Checklist
Making Contact

Set Up a Database

☐ Select the best computer database for you.
- get referrals from other designers
- check with local retailers
- hire a consultant
- use what is integrated with your current project management or word processing programs
- purchase one with preexisting client profile formats
- purchase one you must format yourself

☐ Input all necessary information.
- make it specific
- keep it manageable

Research New Clients

☐ Choose from these six major areas to start your information search:
- Daily newspaper business section
- Office or industrial park directories
- Magazine editorial calendars
- Trade shows
- Design annuals
- Business directories

Identify Contact Person

Once you have information on a company you want to work with, the next step is to identify the individual with the responsibility and the authority to hire you. See page 43 for how to write a script to make this initial call go more smoothly.

Make the Appointment

Use a script, such as the one on page 44, to make the most of this call by helping the potential client decide whether or not he needs your services.

Present Your Portfolio

Use this meeting as more of a consultation than a presentation, so you can discuss the client's needs and how you can meet them.

☐ These three guidelines will help you help your client:
- Reintroduce yourself. Remind him of how you searched out his company and what you believe to be his needs. Now is when he can update your impressions.
- Go "behind the scenes" when showing your portfolio. Share the who, what, when and why behind each piece.

☐ Remember to follow up, during and after the meeting. In other words, determine "next steps" before you leave. Then complete them.

☐ Ask for a referral.

Chapter Four
Working With Clients

S T E P   O N E

Understand the client/
designer relationship.

●

S T E P   T W O

Set the tone
for pricing.

●

S T E P   T H R E E

Show the project's worth.

In this chapter, you will learn to identify what clients are really looking for when they hire a designer they have never worked with before— you! Because this relationship is *not* an employer/ employee one, the rules are much less clearly defined for your clients. With employees, there are hiring practices and labor laws. But there is no "client school" where your clients learn how to hire you, any more than there are traditional classes that teach you how to sell to them. In this chapter you will also learn how to get paid what a job is worth, one of the most important aspects of working with clients. The way you handle the quoting of your first job with them will dictate the nature of your entire relationship!

Understand the Client/ Designer Relationship

When hiring a designer the purpose any client has is to meet their needs at that time. Unlike hiring you as an employee, working with you is a relationship the client can terminate easily—they simply don't call for their next job. A good working relationship between a client and designer often starts at the moment the client is looking for a designer other than the ones they are currently familiar with. The worst time for a client to look for a designer is when they are in a "crunch" and really need one, so most clients have some kind of "short list" of people or firms they have spent time evaluating. Often, you can use this as an opening for a relationship. You can introduce yourself to a prospective client on the basis that you be considered for their "short list." Here are some of the factors clients will evaluate when making the decision to add you to their list.

Expertise

Don't confuse expertise with experience. Expertise is your skill and experience is the application of that skill. Though some clients will insist on someone that has done exactly their kind of job before (and has the experience), most clients are open to trying new talents or different firms based on their ability to demonstrate their expertise. Whether it is packaging design or a newsletter, the prospective client needs to know you can do the work. Experience and expertise make a powerful package, and also a more expensive one!

Compatibility

A certain level of "like to like" is necessary for a successful client/designer relationship. The prospective client will evaluate (both consciously and subconsciously) how you approach them in the first place, how you communicate your interest in their needs, and how you demonstrate flexibility in making appointments or producing estimates.

Professionalism

Probably the most critical aspect of professionalism is your ability to meet deadlines and budgets. You can see the prospective client's dilemma. How can they tell from your phone call, portfolio or promotional piece that you can produce on demand? The best way to establish this fact is through testimonials and references from current clients. You also exhibit professionalism in the appearance of your portfolio and promotions, per-sonal style and appearance, being on time for appointments, consistency in your follow-up, and the presentation of thorough cost proposals.

Communication

You need to clearly and concisely describe your understanding of the prospective client's needs and your ability to meet them with comprehensible and achievable solutions. The most successful relationships depend on this quickness and clarity of communication.

Added Value

What makes you special? Most prospective clients assume technical ability and a certain amount of creativity in designers they might consider working with. What extra services can you provide to make the work easier, faster, better? Clients really want you to solve their headaches, not make more for them!

The Law Says. . . .

Since the 1978 change in the Federal copyright law, the issue of usage must be dealt with when selling your creative services. The current law states that copyright belongs to the creator and use of the work must be transferred by contract. (Note: Concepts or ideas are not protected by law.) The spirit of this law is to invest you, the creator, with control over the profitability of what you create. The exception lies with staff designers whose efforts are considered work for hire. The employer owns the copyright.

When you sell your design services, you are actually selling a portion of the control, i.e., usage, of your work. These usage rights must be clearly stated at the beginning of any relationship. If no rights are stated, then no rights are transferred, and your client has paid for the pleasure of working with you! You can imagine the relationship problems. If no rights are transferred and the client's boss decides to use the design for another project, you may be forced to bill them or (worse case) sue for copyright violation. It is much better to work these details out at the beginning of the relationship when price is discussed.

Copyright Basics

1. Unless otherwise specified, the creator (you) own the copyright.

2. The life of a copyright is your lifetime plus fifty years.

3. The copyright (think "right to copy") is separate from ownership of any originals created.

4. Copyright begins at the moment of tangible expression, also called fixed form.

5. Copyright = Control. This control has two parts. Control can be *exclusive* (no other client may use the work) or *nonexclusive* (other clients may buy use of the work). Control can also be *unlimited* (client does anything he wants) or *limited* (use is limited to a particular usage, such as an annual report or package). Use the following language on your estimates and invoices to protect both you and your client: Exclusive/Unlimited, Exclusive/Limited, Nonexclusive/Unlimited, or Nonexclusive/Limited.

6. Add any of the following to point five to further define the degree of control (usage) your client is purchasing: length of time, geographic territory or place, and size of print run. No rights transferred are no rights received by your client!

7. Copyright registration is not required to own copyright but is required to file a copyright litigation. The copyright notice is not required to keep your copyright, but serves as a "no trespassing" sign! It should be placed on all artwork and used in reproduction of your work whenever possible. For some very easy-to-use pamphlets on this subject, contact the Copyright office (202) 707-9100 and ask for bibliography of forms and publications.

STEP 2 Set the Tone for Pricing

To get off on the right foot with a new client, consider the concepts below. (Note: Everything you do and say at the beginning will be carved in stone and very difficult to change later. If you currently have clients that are difficult to work with, see chapter six.)

Remain Objective

Remove the "you" from the picture when price comes up. It is difficult to price "yourself." Talk about what the annual report or the brochure is worth. Putting yourself in the pricing picture hurts the relationship because it reduces your objectivity.

Use Standard Forms

Use standard industry forms with legally accepted terms and conditions. Don't reinvent the wheel! Get your relationship off to a professional and businesslike start by acting that way! If you haven't purchased the most recent *Graphic Artist's Guild Handbook of Pricing & Ethical Guidelines* (available from North Light Books), do it today. Each edition is updated, and you want to be certain to use the most current forms. Make it easy to accomplish this part of the process of working with clients. The rest is difficult enough! In addition, the American Institute of Graphic Arts (New York) publishes standard forms for estimating and invoicing.

Understand the Situation

Determine at the beginning if you are in a competitive or comparative pricing relationship. In a competitive bid, the client (often a government contract) hires the low bidder, no exceptions. In a comparative situation, the best person or firm for the project gets the job. Neither relationship is good or bad, just know what kind you are getting into.

Find Out Who Is Really in Charge

Your relationship should be with the person that has both the responsibility to find you and the authority to hire you. It will make a big difference in step three, when you show your client what the project is worth.

Make Sure the Client's Needs Are Clear

Good relationships are built on what the client really needs, not necessarily what they say they want. Classic example: A client calls you in for the first job and asks you to design a direct mail brochure. If you don't determine their final objective, you could damage the relationship in the initial meeting or concept stage. Let's say you ask, "What is your purpose, goal or objective? Whom do you want to reach? What do you want people to do when they receive this mailer?" If the answer is, "We want everyone in this particular section of the industry to recognize our name," then, that goal might be better met by designing a trade magazine ad, not a mailer! The mistake (even if it is the client's) would be blamed on you.

Know Business Practices

Know your industry business practices and standards. Read the Joint Ethics Committee Code of Ethics Sidebar, opposite. If a client starts off abusing you on price or copyright because of your lack of education, you deserve it!

Marketing & Promoting Your Work

Code of Fair Practice

Relations Between Artists and Buyers

The word "artist" should be understood to include creative people in the field of visual communications, including but not limited to: illustration, graphic design, photography, film and television.

This Code provides the graphic communications industry with an accepted standard of ethics and professional conduct. It presents guidelines for the voluntary conduct of persons in the industry.

Article 1

Negotiations between an artist or the artist's representative and a client should be conducted only through an authorized buyer.

Article 2

Orders or agreements between an artist or representative and buyer should be in writing and must include the specific rights which are being transferred, the fee plus expenses, delivery date, and a summarized description of the work.

Article 3

All changes or additions not due to he fault of the artist or representative should be billed to the buyer as an additional and separate charge.

Article 4

There should be no charges to the buyer, other than authorized expenses, for revisions or retakes made necessary by errors on the part of the artists or artist's representative.

Article 5

If work commissioned by a buyer is postponed or cancelled, a "kill-fee" should be negotiated based on time allotted, effort expended, and expenses incurred. Completed work must be paid for in full. The artwork must be returned promptly to the artist.

Article 6

Alterations must not be made without consulting the artist. Where alterations or retakes are necessary, the artist must be given the opportunity of making such changes.

Article 7

The artist must notify the buyer of any anticipated delay in delivery. Should the artist fail to keep contract through unreasonable delay or non-conformance with agreed specifications, it will be considered a breach of contract by the artist.

Article 8

An artist must not be asked to work on speculation.

Article 9

There should be no secret rebates, discounts, gifts, or bonuses requested by or given to buyers by artists or representatives.

Article 10

Artwork and copyright ownership are vested in the hands of the artist.

Article 11

Original artwork remains the property of the artist unless it is specifically purchased. It is distinct from the purchase of any reproduction rights. *All transactions must be in writing.

Article 12

In cases of copyright transfers, only specified rights are transferred. All unspecified rights remain vested with the artist. *All transactions must be in writing.

Article 13

Commissioned artwork is not to be considered "work for hire."

Article 14

When the price of work is based on limited use and later such work is used more extensively, the artist must receive additional payment.

Article 15

If exploratory work, comprehensives, or preliminary photographs from an assignment are subsequently used for reproduction, the artist's prior permission must be secured and the

Code of Fair Practice

artist must receive fair additional payment.

Article 16

If exploratory work, comprehensives, or photographs are bought from an artist with the intention or possibility that another artist will be assigned to do the finished work, this must be in writing at the time of placing the order.

Article 17

If no transfer of copyright ownership* has been executed, the publisher of any reproduction of artwork shall publish the artist's copyright notice if the artist requests so at the time of agreement.

Article 18

The right to remove the artist's name on published artwork is subject to agreement between artist and buyer.

Article 19

There must be no plagiarism of any artwork.

Article 20

If an artist is specifically requested to produce any artwork during unreasonable working hours, fair additional remuneration must be paid.

Article 21

All artwork or photography submitted as samples to a buyer should bear the name of the artist or artists responsible for the work. An artist must not claim authorship of another's work.

Article 22

All companies and their employees who receive artist portfolios, samples, etc., must be responsible for the return of the portfolio to the artist in the same condition as received.

Article 23

An artist entering into an agreement with a representative, studio, or production company for an exclusive representation must not accept an order from nor permit work to be shown by any other representative or studio. Any agreement which is not intended to be exclusive should set forth in writing the exact restrictions agreed upon between the two parties.

Article 24

No representative should continue to show an artist's sample after the termination of an association.

Article 25

After termination of an association between artist and representative, the representative should be entitled to a commission for a period of six months on accounts which the representative has secured, unless otherwise specified by contract.

Article 26

Examples of an artist's work furnished to a representative or submitted to a prospective buyer shall remain the property of the artist, should not be duplicated without the artist's consent, and must be returned promptly to artist in good condition.

Article 27

Contests for commercial purposes are not approved of because of their speculative and exploitative character.

Article 28

Interpretation of the Code for the purposes of mediation and arbitration shall be in the hands of the Joint Ethics Committee and is subject to changes and additions at the discretion of the parent organizations through their appointed representatives on the Committee.

*Artwork ownership, copyright ownership, and ownership and right transfers after January 1, 1978 are to be in compliance with the Federal Copyright Revision Act of 1976.

—The Joint Ethics Committee Code of Fair Practice for the Graphics Communication Industry.

Formulated in 1948 in New York City.

STEP 3 Show the Project's Worth

In the present economy, better cost proposals can be the difference between getting the job or not. The increase in jobs put out "to bid" by a client means more competition and closer scrutiny of each and every job expense. Presentation of a thorough cost estimate that illustrates your professionalism, expertise and ability to stay within budgets and meet deadlines can help the client decide to hire you and make sure you get paid what you are worth. As a designer, you have two conflicting goals. One, give your client what they want at the price they want. Two, get the work you want, cover all expenses and make a profit.

To see the best way to present your cost proposals, let's "walk-through" an estimate from start to finish.

Project Description

As part of the detailed project description, you should answer the following questions:

1. What exactly is the assignment?

2. What are the assignment parameters?

3. What is the client's objective(s)?

4. When will this design be presented to the client?

5. Who will see it? Toward what purpose?

6. What will the client supply (copy, photos, illustrations) or provide and when?

7. What are your responsibilities?

Expenses

Itemized expenses can only be estimated, and your form should state that the client agrees to pay actual expenses. Come to some agreement as to how much leeway you have. Industry standard of 10 percent is fine for some clients but would ruin the job for others. State *clearly* what your proposal does *not* include (such as endless comps or printing) so that your client knows what other information is needed for a complete cost estimate.

Changes/Revisions

You should also state what your client will pay for any changes or revisions to the original job description. So, the more detailed the description, the less you risk absorbing any of these expenses!

Advances and Deposits

Discuss advances and deposits. An advance is up-front payment of out-of-pocket expenses. A deposit is a way to get part of your total billing faster than billing for the entire job at the end.

Billing

All invoices should be billed "net receipt." That is, your invoice is considered due when the client's bookkeeping department gets it. This should result in payment within thirty days. Quote a late payment charge on all jobs. Remember, the right to use your work is based on full payment, so your client *should* be highly motivated to pay you! It is customary to state that the client shall also be responsible for all legal fees if late payment has to be resolved legally.

Cancellation Charges

A schedule of cancellation charges is also traditional. Check your association's recommended contract for the exact percentage charges.

Miscellaneous

In addition, existing association estimate forms include a number of conditions based on legal protections you need, such as copyright, credit lines, indemnity and arbitration. These can be picked up verbatim from your association contracts and added to your proposal.

Unless you know you already have the job, it is not enough to submit a standard estimate confirmation with all the legal terms and conditions. Presenting an accurate and binding contract is important, but it is often necessary to add materials to convince the client to pay you what you want. After all, you have told them what it would cost to hire you, but

Show the Project's Worth

not why. Here are some additional elements to add to your cost proposal.

Cover Letter

A good cover letter should warm up an otherwise cold-looking contract and encourage your client to give you the job. Here is an example:

Dear (client's first name),

As we discussed, enclosed is our cost estimate for your "Menu Recipe" packaging designs. In addition, you'll find the design samples you requested to show your supervisor.

You'll find our expertise in this style of design will help you meet your budgets, deadlines and quality controls. We have been working for food industry clients for over five years, and we look forward to providing you with the experience and expertise you need for this project.

Sincerely,

PS—I'll check with you next week to find out when you will be making a final decision on this job. Thank you for your consideration.

Time Line

On design jobs, a time line with your estimate will help a prospective client feel safer in giving you a try. Many clients already have a designer they are working with and you are unknown and untried. You need to make the client feel more comfort-

SUPER STRATEGY
FOURTEEN

How to Avoid Miscommunication

"Invariably conflicts arise as a result of miscommunication. Our Vision Sheet (see page 58) aims to eliminate as much misunderstanding as possible. Not only does it give the designer a better idea of the project's complexities and objectives, but it serves to develop and keep a project's focus for both client and designer. Then, if the client decides that they want to make changes mid-project, showing them their original objectives will force the client to realize that they are changing the direction on which the work was based. This allows us to justify changes in the price of the finished project."

Robert Skrzynski
Q Industria

able! It is always a good idea to use a time line to cover yourself for client approval times as well. If they don't meet their deadlines, you have a better chance of getting yours extended. Example:

May 1   Received information from client

May 10   Concept sketches ready for client selection

May 10   Rough copy due from client

May 15   Final selection of concept due

May 15   Final copy due from client

May 22   Layout ready for approval

May 24   Layout approval due

May 25   Product photo shoot

May 30   Artwork ready for approval

Jun 1   Artwork approval due

Jun 2   Artwork to printer

Jun 10   Color and bluelines from printer

Jun 15   Printing completed

Samples

Finally, include samples of the kind of work you will be doing. Never assume the client will remember the work they saw in your portfolio or promotion materials. Count on having to visually reestablish your professional credentials. This will help you get your price, because you have shown you can do the work requested. Also, samples will help your client help you get the job when it's time to present your quote for scrutiny by a committee that has never met you or seen your portfolio!

SUPER STRATEGY

FIFTEEN

Make Your Proposals Complete

"We care so much about clients. When you have a conflict, it is personally painful, so we work like the devil to make sure it won't happen. If we think something like pricing or copyright may become an issue, we cover it in the proposal. We also refer clients to the *Graphic Artist's Guild Handbook of Pricing & Ethical Guidelines*. It helps if they don't think you are being arbitrary."

Lynn Donham
Church Street Design

Chapter Four Checklist
Working With Clients

Make sure you understand what clients are really looking for when they hire a particular designer for the first time.

STEP 1 Understand the Client/ Designer Relationship

☐ Review the following "hiring considerations." Where would you fall on a scale of one to ten (one = very weak; ten = very strong) if you ranked yourself in each area?

- Expertise. This is your skill at doing something, not your experience. The client has to feel confident that you can do the job, regardless of your years of experience as a designer.
- Compatibility. The initial, and ongoing, impression you make on a potential client is critical. Whether or not you agree with their importance in actually doing the job, compatibility and *likability* influence a client's decision to hire you.
- Professionalism. You must be able to meet deadlines and stay within budgets. Use client testimonials and references to help convince a prospect of your ability to be professional.
- Communication. You must clearly and concisely describe your client's needs and offer comprehensible and achievable solutions.
- Added Value. What extra services can you provide to make the work easier, faster and better?

☐ Make absolutely sure you understand the rights of ownership to your work as they are spelled out in the Copyright Law of 1978. Review page 55 to get up to speed in this area.

STEP 2 Set the Tone for Pricing

☐ Keep in mind these six concepts when undertaking pricing, especially when doing so with a first-time client.

- Remove the "you" from the picture. Instead, talk about what the project is worth.
- Use standard industry forms with legally accepted terminology and conditions. Purchase the current Graphic Artists Guild *Handbook of Pricing & Ethical Guidelines*.
- Make sure you know if you are in a competitive or comparative pricing situation. See page 56 for definitions of these terms.
- Find out who is really in charge. This is the person you should be working with, if at all possible.
- Be certain you have clearly identified the client's needs. Don't go just on what they tell you their needs are. They may be wrong. Probe and dig from all angles: What is their objective? Who do they want to reach? What action do they want from the recipient?
- Know industry business practices and standards. With the availability of copyright information and Code

of Ethics information (see pages 57-58), you have no excuse if you are ever taken advantage of.

STEP 3 · Show the Project's Worth

Putting together a thorough cost estimate illustrates your professionalism, expertise and ability to stay within budgets and meet deadlines.

☐ These are the first questions your estimate should answer:

- What is the design project? Who is the audience? What is the client's objective(s)?
- When will the design solution be presented to the client?
- Who will participate in this presentation? What roles will they play?
- What materials (copy, photos, illustrations) will the client supply?
- What are your responsibilities?

☐ These are the major areas that your estimates must always cover:

- Expenses. The client should pay actual expenses, not what you estimate them to be.
- Changes/Revisions. Be clear about what changes or revisions will cost the client.
- Advances and deposits. Arranging for these will ensure that you are paid for out-of-pocket expenses in advance and that a portion of your billing will be paid sooner than the end of the project.

- Billing. Your invoices should be billed "net receipt," which means the bill is due when the client's accounting department receives it. This should result in payment within thirty days.
- Cancellation Charges. A schedule of cancellation charges is traditional.
- Miscellaneous. Check the *Graphic Artist's Guild Handbook of Pricing & Ethical Guidelines* for legal protection conditions covering copyright, credit lines, arbitration and indemnity that you should include.

☐ Always attach a cover letter to "warm up" and humanize your estimate.

☐ Add a time line to make a client more comfortable about your professionalism.

☐ Include samples of your work with the estimate to visually reestablish your expertise.

Chapter Five
Getting Repeat Business

S T E P   O N E

Make Your Clients
Want to Stay.

●

S T E P   T W O

Use business-building
techniques.

●

S T E P   T H R E E

Learn to work with
out-of-town clients.

In today's marketplace, when can you be satisfied that you now have a regular client? The best answer is, "Never!" Never plan on clients coming back; you must create a plan to *keep* them coming back. This chapter will help you establish supportive relationships with your clients. It will help you create promotional items that your clients will be able to use and that will show clients what you can do for them.

STEP 1 Make Your Clients Want

You know that you're not really selling design services, you are selling design *solutions*. What does this mean from the client's perspective? What are your clients really buying from you? Consider the ten points below the next time you are making any kind of client presentation. Integrating these points into your sales presentations will help give your clients specific and tangible reasons to work with you—instead of a competitor!

Demonstrate Your Technical Ability

Clients are buying your expertise to take them from point *A* to point *B*. Often, they know what they want, but not how to get it. That's your job! Use every opportunity you can to demonstrate your technical abilities to your clients. Most often, you can endear a client to you by making something they don't understand (or want to understand) look easy to do.

Match Goals With Your Client

Be absolutely certain, especially on the first job, that you know whether the client wants a creative collaboration with you or simply to have you document and record the information they give you. This matching of objectives creates the compatibility that brings clients back for more work with you. The lack of attention to this detail can lead to the loss of future business as well as problems with the job itself.

Make Them Look Good

Whether you are dealing with the owner or an employee of the business, your client has to answer to someone or achieve some objective through the work they do with you. You can make your clients want to stay with you by a continual awareness of how the success of your work together will make them look to *their* clients or bosses. Become partners with your client!

Help Your Client Overcome Frustrations and Meet Challenges

Today's marketplace has put tremendous pressure on your clients. Often, one person is doing the work of three, or bosses are demanding they get the same work from you for less money. Do what you can on each job to make sure you are helping your client meet the demands of his job.

Be Flexible

Clients need you to be flexible in reaching the final results on any project. This does not mean you need to drop your price or do free work; it's more of an attitude. Even to say, "We're flexible, we're here to get you there" is reassuring to your clients.

Deal Directly With Budgets and Deadlines

There probably aren't two more hotly contested issues between clients and designers than getting the project

done on time and within budget. Your job really consists of two parts. One, make sure the client doesn't stray from the original job description in terms of the money they're spending with you, and two, make sure they get their approvals in on time so you can meet the deadline. This is often difficult in the "heat" of the creative process, but you must be the one to put on the brakes and stay on track. No matter what is said during the project, you'll be the one blamed for a late job or an over-budget invoice, so you must stay in control. It may be hard to do at the time, but your client will (probably silently) thank you for it later.

Make It Easy for Your Client to Stay

Be sure there are no physical obstacles to keep a client from coming back. Your client should not have a lot of difficulty in reaching you by phone (a common complaint by clients). They should be able to find your studio easily if they have to meet with you there (a map would be nice!). Smooth the way.

Be Trustworthy

Help your client understand that they can trust you to produce and deliver a professional design project that will meet their need on time. Your client's biggest fear is that they may have hired the wrong designer for the project. Unlike buying tangi-

to Stay

ble goods, they can't examine the brochure before you deliver it! Be sensitive to their concerns.

Help Increase Productivity

Every client needs to work more productively to make the kind of profits they need to stay in business. How can working with you or your firm help them do that? One way is to look at every project from a "multiple usage" basis. Be concerned as to how the client could use the work you are producing for more than a one-time purpose. Not only will this help add value to working with you, but it also could lead to future work together!

Help Increase Profitability

Clients are more sensitive to the bottom line, not only on a per-project basis but in the overall sense of increasing their company profits. They will be more likely to come back and work with you if you can help them figure out how to either decrease their overhead or increase their sales. Every project can be examined from this perspective. Even if you cannot make any positive suggestions, the client will know you tried.

SUPER STRATEGY

SIXTEEN

Establish a Supportive Relationship

"We believe that our clients come back to us because of timely, well-executed work and our family orientation. We provide unusual creativity. We integrate concepts in all work for longevity. Our clients feel like they are getting their money's worth when they work with us.

"We are a family-oriented group. We've been with some of our clients since we started. Clients become a part of the family. We involve our clients. We do projects with our clients, not for them. And, we work with people we really enjoy ... it is almost a mutual interview process. Most of our clients are great to share ideas and projects with. A lot of good ideas come from our clients, which we incorporate into their pieces."

Eric and Jack Boelts
Boelts Brothers Design

SUPER STRATEGY

SEVENTEEN

Give Clients Something They Can Use

"Promotions should be so special that people will want to keep them. So many artists just do postcards, but many design firms just throw them away. I do handmade pieces with texture . . . so cool and precious . . . no one will throw them away.

"I do three to four promos per year. Small runs of 250. All are handmade and are very labor-intensive. Distribution is through the mail. I send the first one hundred to my existing clients for them to keep. The second batch goes to people I want to work with. I use the American Institute of Graphic Arts list or purchase a list. Ninety percent of my mailings are to AIGA members. I send my pieces to members I dream of working with. Sometimes I get names from magazines. I send samples of my work to designers whose work I like.

"My most recent is called 'The Year of the Dog.' It is an embossed, blank book with three illustrations or plates of dogs. The job is three-color and was developed as a New Year's promo. This promo piece can be used for notes also. It's in the shape of a reporter's pad. The Year of the Dog got a great

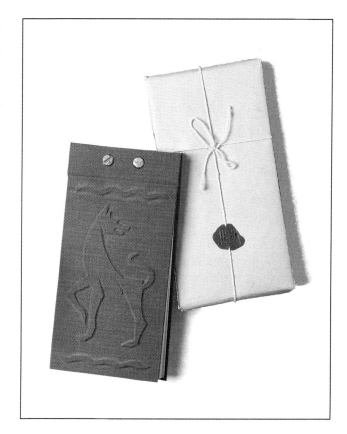

reaction. It prompted people to ask for more samples of my work. It has resulted in several jobs and referrals. The promo has already paid for itself."

Lynn Tanaka
Lynn Tanaka Illustration

STEP 2 Use Business-Building Techniques

It's clear that the best source for new business is still the last client you worked with. It can be five to ten times more expensive to be constantly looking for new clients as it is to keep the ones you already have. This can increase your profitability because repeat business can reduce expenses for self-promotion!

You won't keep all of your clients. Some will have an unsatisfactory (real or perceived) experience. Some will not be able to keep up with your growth as a business when you charge more for your experience, and they will drop off the bottom of your client list as you bring in new business. Some will simply want to try a different style of work (don't take it personally). Here are some suggestions for building repeat business.

Provide Basic Client Services in Your Studio

Physical comfort is important when clients have to visit your space and spend any time there. Can they make private phone calls? Have access to a fax machine? Eat a decent meal if they stay for lunch? No, these don't have anything to do with design, but have everything to do with service.

Maintain Regular Contact

Improve nonselling communication with your clients by contacting them outside your regular sales calls. For example, send them articles you think they would find interesting or suggest going to seminars together. Spending nonselling time on your clients builds the relationship that builds repeat business.

Immerse Yourself in Their Industry

Go to their trade shows, subscribe to their industry publications. The more you know about the business your client is in, the more successful you will be together.

Follow Up After the Project

Make a "project follow-up" call after the work you delivered has been in use for some time. Ask the question, "How is that booth graphic working?" or "What was the response on that mailer?" In other words, you are asking, "How did it work for you?" Three answers you need to know can come from this kind of call: (1) are there any unanticipated problems that need to be resolved; (2) is there a possibility of another job together; and (3) is your job done—is that brochure, mailer, etc., working for the client as it was supposed to?

Collaborate for Publicity

Get your client to invest in your success together. For example: enter design awards with them, write project media releases together, even do cooperative motion pieces. Become a creative partnership.

Keep Clients Up-To-Date

Often clients hire you for something very specific and are not aware of your other "marketing messages" or services. Be sure to keep your clients up-to-date on new projects and services you have to offer.

Remind Them to Reorder

Another great technique to guarantee repeat business is to track the use of the work you do for clients on a regular basis (such as data sheets for trade shows or the reprinting of their product catalog), and call them before they call you to remind them it's time to reorder! Not only will this increase your value to the client, but you create jobs for yourself or your firm on a regular basis.

Keep Questions Open-Ended

Finally, keep the questions your clients ask on an "open-ended" status and continue to provide them with updates as new information becomes available. For example, a client may ask you about measuring ad response. After answering the question, watch for articles on this topic in trade publications and send copies to your client.

SUPER STRATEGY

EIGHTEEN

Send Out Christmas Cards

"In keeping with my personal approach, I design my own Christmas cards. These cards are my way of keeping in touch with clients I may only speak to once a year, and a way of reinforcing my current contacts or even making new ones. Like everything else I do, they are an extension of my personality. I try to make them unique, but most of all, interesting to me.

They always result in calls. I also send out twenty-dollar bottles of champagne to selected clients. The twenty-dollar figure is within the legal limit and not large enough to be misunderstood. It makes quite an impression. I can't think of another gift that would attract as much attention for the same amount of money. It also makes me stick out, as few people bother to give gifts. Being memorable has gotten me work."

Michael Pilla
Michael Pilla Design

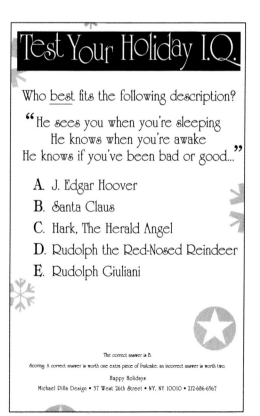

Test Your Holiday I.Q.

Who **best** fits the following description?

"He sees you when you're sleeping
He knows when you're awake
He knows if you've been bad or good..."

A. J. Edgar Hoover
B. Santa Claus
C. Hark, The Herald Angel
D. Rudolph the Red-Nosed Reindeer
E. Rudolph Giuliani

The correct answer is B.

Scoring: A correct answer is worth one extra piece of fruitcake, an incorrect answer is worth two.

Happy Holidays
Michael Pilla Design • 37 West 26th Street • NY, NY 10010 • 212-686-6567

Fa LaLa La LaLa La La La

Wishing You A Joyous Holiday And A Happy New Year

Michael Pilla & Associates • 19 West 44th Street • New York, NY 10036 • 212-768-8646
Desk Top Design for Marketing and Promotion

STEP 3 Learn to Work With Out-of-Town Clients

Traditionally, designers and design firms have depended on their local market for new business through sales strategies, referrals and word-of-mouth marketing. Now, and in the future, the competition and the economy dictate a more aggressive approach. The effort to bring in new business from out-of-town clients can be summarized with the old standard, "Plan the work and work the plan."

First be sure you have an overall plan for the local market, often called "bread and butter" clients, before going after the bigger (but harder to get) national clients. The national clients and projects, almost by definition, are bigger with better budgets. After all, for a client in St. Louis to hire a designer from San Francisco for their annual report requires a level of style and service that the client feels they can't necessarily get from a St. Louis designer.

When you make the decision to pursue out-of-town clients, sell yourself as offering a unique and distinctly different style. You can't try to sell someone else's formula or style.

One Selling Strategy That Worked

When Marty Neumeier started his own firm in 1973, there were no other design firms listed in the telephone book for his area. Traditional word-of-mouth marketing worked well at the time. By 1979, there were more than thirty firms listed and Marty decided it was time to develop a more aggressive plan for bringing new clients to the studio. Marty knew he wanted new clients on a more regional and national level as well as more work from existing local clients. Because finding new clients means knowing what you are looking for in order to know where to look, Marty found himself faced with the three choices any designer has for targeting new business. He could focus on a specific industry (such as financial services or high-tech), a type of design project (such as packaging or annual reports), or a particular style of design. Obviously, targeting by industry or project is easier in the local market because the potential clients are easy to identify. Financial companies can be researched through industry directories. Annual report projects can be found from publicly held companies. Style, on the other hand, is very subjective and it is a more difficult area for new business development. But Marty decided that this was the best approach for contacting out-of-town clients!

First, Marty defined his style. What will a client get from Neumeier Design they wouldn't get from any other design firm? After six intense months of self-evaluation, he came up with the "Neumeier Philosophy"—he would give his clients whole design and not the more traditional piecemeal or project approach. Many designers will design, produce and print a client's brochure without reference to the rest of the firm's advertising and collateral materials. Marty decided he wanted to work with clients that needed everything from their corporate identity to their packaging to work together as a total and complete package. This meant fewer jobs but bigger jobs and clients with the ability and security to put everything in the hands of one designer. In addition, Marty could support his philosophy by offering his personal style for all creative aspects. He is designer, illustrator and copywriter. Everything would have his distinctive individual imprint.

After defining what he is selling, Marty's next challenge was to ascertain who would buy it. After months of further investigation, he came up with the following profile of a potential client for his style:

1. Their product or service would be somewhat unique or unusual. These firms would be spiritually closer to his own unique approach because of their own originality.

Learn to Work With Out-of-Town Clients

2. Because of its uniqueness, the firm would be less conservative and traditional and more open to innovative marketing approaches.

3. The firm would have a very high quality consciousness. They would believe in quality over quantity.

4. The firm would have to be small enough where design decisions were not split among different, unconnected departments. But not too small that it couldn't afford better-quality production.

Now that Marty had determined what and who, all that remained was how to reach these people and get the work! He started with an idea that his style could not be described in a traditional design promo piece. No postcard or flyer would be able to fully communicate his comprehensive approach. Also, the format of the piece would help self-select potential clients. That is, people that liked his promotion would probably like working with him. He designed, produced and printed an eighty-page softcover, four-color book. He did it all—design, illustration and writing—much like he would do for a client. He designed it to both impress and inform.

He designed it with very high production values to position himself as "good enough" to the national client. Marty felt the physical nature of the piece would attract the client he had profiled. Marty's book cost $20,000 for 1,000 copies. He matched his high-level goals (national clients) with a high level of money and effort to get the work. The book became his promo piece, portfolio and his rep. It told potential clients everything they would need to know to get them interested.

Marty found potential clients by studying the business section of the local paper and the *Wall Street Journal*. He then sent the book to these clients that fit his profile and followed up with a call to discuss the client's response. When he first started using the book for new business development, it brought in $40,000 in new business. Most of all, it brought national recognition and new clients from as far away as California and Minnesota, New York and Nebraska. Though it was expensive, it was the perfect object for his immediate launch into the national arena. Next, Marty looked for a consistent and low-cost method of updating the information in his book and showcasing current work for clients. Deliberately designed as a "one-use" piece, the book could not be remailed to the same clients. Also, the binding prevented physically updating the book. He followed the book with a news release-style design. The base piece was two-color, sized $7'' \times 10\frac{1}{2}''$, and printed in quantities of 5,000 with name and logo masthead and blank body. These were then warehoused at the printer for the convenience of the frequent printing schedule. Then, Marty wrote a media release about current awards won or projects and had the printer run one-color printing onto the existing logo-printed stock. These releases worked on an ongoing basis because they were flexible, affordable, easy to use. The regular mailings tell clients and potential clients that the Neumeier Philosophy is alive and well and working. As an additional bonus, individual releases were bound (he uses a standard plastic comb binding) and sent to clients that need specific information. For example, Marty quickly and easily can bind and send all the releases related to packaging when a client is looking at just that particular capability. Or, he can create an instant mini-book by binding a selection of twenty or thirty existing releases that reflect the Neumeier Philosophy.

Marty identified his out-of-town potential clients, then developed a campaign to get their business. This process alone demonstrated to his potential clients that the Neumeier Philosophy could work for them as well. Now, in today's new economy and marketplace, his firm has changed their marketing strategy from selling style to industry-specific—computer and software clients. Today, Neumeier Design Team focuses on retail packaging for software and hardware companies.

SUPER STRATEGY

NINETEEN

Year-at-a-Glance Calendar Promotion

"I have done a Year-at-a-Glance calendar for the past six years, and it has been very successful and well received. The format is the same from year to year, yet I invite a different illustrator or photographer to participate each time. Then, the artist, myself and the printer all use the calendars in our own marketing efforts as a three-way trade for talent and services.

"The benefits as a promo piece are: (1) It is a useful item for clients, not just another postcard. (2) Shelf life is one year. (3) It is small, compact, and easy to ship. (4) I have designed it to be easy to use as a real calendar. Each year I print 1,000 and mail 500 to clients, prospective clients and fellow professionals in my network. I use the balance of 500 as promos throughout the year. I feel pretty confident that the success of the piece has a lot to do with mailing in January to avoid the holiday rush."

Jeanine Colini
Jeanine Colini Design Associates

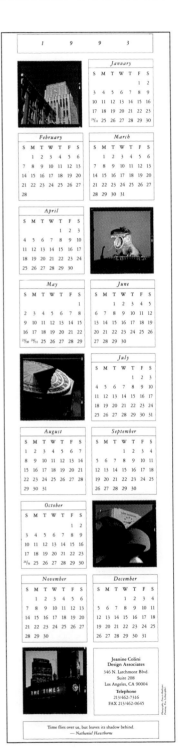

SUPER STRATEGY

TWENTY

Holiday Promotions That Work All Year

"We believe that we control the volume of the message we are communicating to clients. It is up to us as designers to turn on the communication and pump up the volume. One method that has been successful in this effort has been our annual holiday promotion. It is not filled with information about our firm, our awards or accomplishments. The word *gift* more aptly describes our approach. Our list always seems to include clients, friends, vendors, and even our competitors. Rarely do we target new clients at this time. It is not a new business development piece.

"Though the holiday promotions are always well received, they are often displayed where a secondary audience comes into contact with our name and our work. Beyond that, the third audience results from our entering the pieces into design competitions. These awards have built our reputation and have gotten us new clients. This is an example of turning up the volume.

"The No Nos poster promotion was quite

successful for us. We wanted to communicate a very simple idea in a very simple, yet clever, manner. The poster included a one-line message, 'May the answers to all your holiday wishes be yes.' The image used to convey this message was two large 'No' symbols (circle with a diagonal bar). Each canceled the other out. In other words, we wish you 'No Nos.'

"The tongue-in-cheek message and the humorous approach of the Santa Barbara poster gave all of our clients a chuckle. The image, a likeness of then First Lady Barbara Bush dressed up like Santa, was screen printed in four matched colors. When we sent a copy to Mrs. Bush, we were pleased when she wrote us back thanking us for the gift. The poster won several awards and was published in three national design publications."

Keith Puccinelli
Puccinelli Design

Chapter Five Checklist
Getting Repeat Business

You can never count on a client automatically coming back with more work. You must have a plan for getting repeat business.

STEP 1
Make Your Clients Want to Stay

☐ Demonstrate your technical ability at every opportunity. You can endear yourself to a client by making something they don't understand look easy.

☐ Match goals with your client. Know whether a client wants to collaborate creatively with you or wants you to document and record the information they give you.

☐ Make them look good. Always be aware of how the success of your working together will make your client look good to *their* clients or bosses.

☐ Help your client overcome frustrations and meet challenges. Do whatever you can to help your client meet the demands of their job.

☐ Be flexible in your attitude and your dealings with a client.

☐ Deal directly with budgets and deadlines. Part of your job is to make sure the client doesn't stray from the original project description and to make sure they get their approvals in on time. The other part is to make sure you do the same!

☐ Make it easy for your client to stay. Remove all physical barriers between you and your client, such as busy telephones (get two lines or call waiting) and incomplete road directions to your studio (supply a map).

☐ Be trustworthy. Be sensitive to client concerns and never, ever do anything to undermine your client's trust.

☐ Help increase productivity. Look at every project from a "multiple usage" basis. How can the client maximize his investment in your work?

☐ Help increase profitability. Clients will be more likely to come back if you somehow help them either decrease their overhead or increase revenue.

STEP 2
Use Business-Building Techniques

Provide your visiting clients with essential business services: privacy, faxing, beverages, lunch, photocopying, etc.

☐ Spend nonselling time keeping in touch with clients.

☐ Immerse yourself in your client's business. Go to trade shows. Subscribe to industry publications.

☐ Make project follow-up calls to see if a design solution worked for the client.

☐ Get your client to invest in your success together through collaborative public relations or contest submissions.

☐ Keep your clients up-to-date on new projects and services you offer.

☐ Track the use of work you've completed (e.g., catalogs, letterhead, etc.) and contact the client to remind them to reorder.

☐ Keep the line of communication open-ended by continually updating a client on a topic of mutual interest.

STEP 3
Learn to Work With Out-of-Town Clients

The effort to bring in new business from out of town can be summarized with the old standard, "Plan the work and work the plan."

☐ Have a plan for marketing locally (your bread-and-butter clients) before going after bigger (and tougher) national clients.

☐ Learn from your peers who have already conquered this territory. Also, read the story on page 71 about designer Marty Neumeier and how he made it to the big time.

Chapter Six
Managing Conflict

S T E P   O N E

Sell your ideas
to the client.

●

S T E P   T W O

Turn problem clients into
profitable clients.

Now that you have gotten the word out—clients are calling you and you have great working relationships with clients that come back—what's next? Having a plan to deal with client conflicts and problems is a good idea! The worst time to come up with a conflict management plan is when you are right in the middle of a conflict! If you can successfully resolve a conflict and as a result make your client feel really good about you, you have made inroads in creating a profitable relationship.

STEP 1 Sell Your Ideas to the Client

In general, you know that approaching design jobs means proposing your idea as the solution to an objective your client wants to meet. You can avoid many conflicts with clients by carefully evaluating the situation before you present your idea to the client, and by keeping a watchful eye on the presentation itself. Here are some suggestions for making careful and thorough ongoing analyses:

Never Take a Situation at "Face Value"

What the client thinks the solution should be and what you think may be two different viewpoints. For example, the client is rushed and pressed for time and tells you to go ahead on a change order without an estimate amendment. *Stop!* If you go ahead and pursue the change without an updated cost approval, you can be certain the client will end up asking, "Where did these extra charges come from?" Little matter that you can say they told you to go ahead without regard to cost. Trust your instincts. Cost (and any other problem/solution situation) will always be important to the client—after the job! If you go ahead and do the work regardless of cost and it fails to meet the client's "hidden agenda," who will be blamed? You!

Be Clear, Complete and Conscientious

Be as specific and focused as possible when proposing your idea and what it will accomplish. Leave no gaps that might turn into ambiguities later on.

Support Your Solutions

Present success stories of what similar solutions have done for other firms. Use published articles on relevant topics to support these case studies. Some clients need to feel they are not breaking entirely new ground. Use your judgment!

Cover All Costs

What costs are involved to implement your idea? Remember, costs involve not only the dollar investment but the time and energy the client has to authorize. Be sure to cover all three points (time, energy and money) to sell your idea completely. In addition, see North Light Books' recent publication, *Setting the Right Price for Your Design & Illustration.* Then, you are presenting "industry standards" and not just your notion of costs.

Use the Time Line Tool

A time line is helpful when trying to sell a client on a really new approach or idea. If it is something they have never done before, a breakdown of who-does-what-when will help sell them and point out their step-by-step responsibilities.

Know Exactly Who's Involved

Will your proposal be evaluated by a committee? Find out! Many ideas are scrutinized by at least two or more people at your client's firm. You should know the entire cast of characters so you are better able to anticipate possible holdups or hang-ups.

Marketing & Promoting Your Work

STEP 2 Turn Problem Clients Into Profitable Clients

Sometimes, no matter what you do or how much you prepare in advance, problems with clients will develop. Since you know it is less expensive (and more profitable) to keep clients than constantly be out looking for new ones, follow these six points to turn problems into profit:

Identify the Specific Problem

Is the problem objective (the ink isn't what was specified) or subjective (the ink is the specified color, but now the client doesn't like it). The difference is very important since it will dictate the direction your problem resolution will take. An objective problem is measurable and clearly must be corrected. A subjective problem is an opinion and may not need to be fixed by you. Sometimes subjective problems are situations where the client needs to express their opinion and you'll find them happy with one of two solutions: (1) you hear them out, they just want to express an opinion; or (2) you treat the problem as a change order, not as a problem, and the client is charged accordingly.

Review the Job Description

At the front end of the job, you can't get too much job information. If a client hesitates in giving you answers or doesn't know a spec, stop and ask them to find out the information. Use this "no fail" question approach: "Since I'm sure you want this project

---

SUPER STRATEGY

TWENTY-ONE

Stick to Your Contractual Objectives

"Most design firms fail and even encourage conflict at the initial contract stage. Since the esthetics of design are so subjective, our contracts are set up to achieve specific and measurable objectives. In one situation, we were hired to create a corporate image and identity. We worked effectively with the consulting and the research divisions, but then had to resign the account when the client ultimately made an arbitrary selection of an identity that failed to meet the positioning statement agreed to in the consulting and research phases."

Bill Jensen
Jensen Communications

Turn Problem Clients Into Profitable Clients

to be done correctly, when will this information be available?" Speak up and never make an assumption of what the client really needs.

Decide If You Want to Work With This Client Again

The answer will change your approach and attitude. If you plan to continue the relationship, focus on what is objective and measurable and avoid concentrating on personality and blaming. You can change a client's behavior, but not their personality!

Involve the Client in the Solution

Ask them for their opinion and what they would suggest if they were in your position. Ask them for their "wish list" solution and then for something more practical. Get a dialogue going back and forth. The more time and energy (and money) the client invests in deciding the solution, the more likely they'll see it to its resolution and want to work with you again.

Document, Document, Document

Just in case everything falls apart and you have to take any legal action, be sure to document everything step by step. This "paper trail" of work orders and change orders, even phone logs, will serve you well if you can't save the client and keep the problem from being a complete loss or expense to you.

Follow Up

Schedule follow-up once the problem resolution is in place. You want to make sure the problem stays fixed!

SUPER STRATEGY

TWENTY-TWO

Conflict Resolution Checklist

"We have a five-point checklist for dealing with client conflicts.

1. Set up a face-to-face meeting with the client.

2. Be logical and avoid emotional involvement.

3. Determine the client's hot buttons (then avoid them) and what they will respond to.

4. Present the solution, but have a good "plan B" in order to ultimately make the best of the situation.

5. Decide if you want to continue the relationship. Is this a one-time or occasional problem or is it a chronic conflict?"

Trina Gardner-Nouvo

White + Associates

Good Business Ethics

As in any other business, ethical considerations confront design professionals on a daily basis. The key is to be prepared by thinking through the potential situations that could arise and by having some idea of how you would handle them.

Ethics are the characteristics developed for your business that will help you make good behavioral choices. The attributes that are the foundation of ethical behavior include: integrity, honesty, trustworthiness, truthfulness, commitment, awareness or sensitivity to the situation, responsibility, fairness and a sense of compassion.

Being ethical does *not* mean being weak or nonassertive! Ethical behavior is the foundation of good business practices for clients and designers.

Why should you be concerned about your business ethics? Because your clients and other designers will accept your behavior as the basis of your day-to-day ethical business practices. And they will never let you forget it if you behave unethically just one time. Paying attention to ethics is common sense in business. Clients that feel they have been treated unfairly or dishonestly won't come back. And finally, you *feel good* when you do the right thing.

Ethics do not always involve big issues. You are probably making good day-to-day ethical decisions without a second thought, but sometimes it can be the little things that create good business practices and ethics. They become codes of conduct inspired and directed by the feeling of wanting to do "the right thing."

Here are some examples of the day-to-day situations that offer the opportunity for either ethical or unethical behavior. How do you act in these situations?

1. Delivering on every contract, even verbal, whether it is with a client, supplier or vendor.

2. Billing job expenses fairly and getting the markup you need to make a profit while not taking advantage of your client.

3. Maintaining confidentiality in the client/designer relationship. Your client should be able to trust that they can consult with you on their proprietary or restricted products and not have any "leaks" to the outside.

4. Making honest and accurate claims in your advertising and marketing.

5. Dealing fairly in your agency or rep relationships and abiding by the contracts you both agreed to.

As a rule, you know that you are facing an ethical decision when you can identify any of the following three factors:

1. Your personal happiness would be achieved at the expense of fairness or honest treatment of another person.

2. Other people that will be affected by your decision are not considered or consulted.

3. The long-term gain of your decision is taken as a more important consideration than the immediate gain or benefit. In other words, doing the right thing may not yield its benefit right away.

How do you know you are on ethically "thin ice" when you are facing any decision? The best test is to watch for rationalizations you verbalize (or think to yourself) that allow you to move ahead with ethically poor behavior. Here are some common rationalizations:

1. I'm just fighting fire with fire.

2. It's not illegal, is it?

3. Everyone does it.

4. It's just how you play the game.

5. It's OK as long as no one gets hurt.

6. I have to do whatever it takes to get the job.

7. I'll only be as ethical as my competition.

Chapter Six Checklist
Managing Conflict

 STEP 1 Sell Your Ideas to the Client

The best odds for successfully selling your ideas are in recognizing the possibility of conflict and having a means of preventing it.

☐ Avoid conflict by carefully evaluating the project so you are certain what the client needs before you present your design solutions.

☐ Avoid conflict by keeping a watchful eye and ear open for client concerns during the presentation and resolve them immediately.

Specifically:

- Never take a situation at "face value." What the client thinks the solution should be and what you think may be two different things. Never let yourself be rushed or pressured into making a decision or a revision that goes against your instinct or experience.
- Be clear, complete and conscientious when presenting your design solution and how it will perform.
- Support your solutions with success stories or relevant articles.
- Cover all costs—time, energy and money—completely.
- Use the time line tool to show exactly how the process, especially one new to the client, will break down by date and responsibility.
- Know exactly who is involved so you can try to anticipate problems or concerns from the various sectors of the client's company.

 STEP 2 Turn Problem Clients Into Profitable Clients

☐ Identify the specific problem. Is the problem objective (e.g., the printer used the wrong color) or subjective (e.g., the client no longer likes the color they approved)? You can measure and fix objective problems. You may not be able to fix a subjective problem without charging for changes or revisions.

☐ Review the project description. Because you spent the time at the start of the project to get all the facts, you have the detailed description you need to evaluate if a job has gone off track and who is at fault.

☐ Decide if you want to work with this client again. If the answer is yes, look for an objective and measurable solution.

☐ Involve the client in the solution. The more time and money the client invests in deciding the solution, the more likely they will see it implemented.

☐ Document, document, document. Just in case everything falls apart and legal action is indicated, be sure you've documented each and every stage of the relationship and the conflict.

☐ Schedule follow-up once the problem resolution is in place. You want to make sure the problem stays fixed.

Chapter Seven
Hiring Professional Services

STEP ONE

Decide if you need a rep.

●

STEP TWO

Find the right rep.

●

STEP THREE

Hire a marketing
coordinator.

As competition for design assignments increases, many creative professionals feel they need to hire a professional representative or marketing coordinator. Basically, reps work in three important ways to build your design business: They find new clients; they keep those clients coming back; and they negotiate the best pricing and terms with these clients. This chapter will help you decide if you should take this step.

Decide If You Need a Rep

Here are ten guidelines that will help you decide. You need a rep if you:

1. Are too busy with work to make the personal contacts necessary to find new clients and keep the ones you have.

2. Have enough "bread-and-butter" work in a stable client base that allows you to spend money on the additional promotional material reps require.

3. Have a strong style or specialty that a rep can target clients for.

4. Have enough knowledge about how to sell yourself but want someone else to do it.

5. Consider yourself first as a business then as a designer. Reps work best with people that appreciate the "profit-making" nature of their work. Anyone can say they want to be successful, but that means you must have the business education to be in charge of setting your goals and direction. A rep is there to realize your goals, not set them for you.

6. Are willing to spend the time to assist the rep in selling your work. You will not spend less time on your marketing by having a rep. You just won't do the same things. For example, instead of showing the portfolio, you will be creating new portfolio pieces for the rep to show.

7. Are looking for ways to promote your business and need a rep's time and expertise.

8. Practice good business management methods and have a professional attitude toward promotion. Established and efficient project management procedures and policies are important criteria of professionalism required by reps.

9. Have a head start on a portfolio of the kind of work you want to do. With commission sales, no portfolio means "down" time a rep can't afford.

10. Have the marketing plan and budget for your promotion pieces and plans to support the direction you give the rep.

SUPER STRATEGY

TWENTY-THREE

Using Client Posters as Self-Promotion

"One or two of our most successful promo pieces were posters we designed for nonprofit clients. The poster we design becomes a tool for them. It's also a tool for us, because we later enter the poster in design contests. The notoriety we get from entering contests kicks back work. Posters have been incredibly effective. Creative clients will look through design journals. Conservative clients, i.e., marketing directors for banks and the like can't make that leap. So we target our promotions to more creatively minded companies."

Eric and Jack Boelts
Boelts Brother Design

Find the Right Rep

Reps own their own business and represent individuals that have their own businesses. The relationship is that of an "independent contractor" and not employee/employer. The designer contracts with the rep for marketing services and pays approximately 20 to 30 percent of each job fee on all clients in the rep's territory. Territory can defined geographically (local market only) or by type of work (packaging design).

Business or office management often is not part of a rep's job responsibilities because these tasks are overhead activities and don't directly generate commission as sales calls do.

Finding a rep is very similar to the search for clients. You must research the reps, meet with them, and do the regular follow-up required to build a relationship. Reps, like clients, also may already have a designer that does what you do, and good follow-up is the only way to break through this barrier to working together. Knowing who the rep already works with allows you to approach them in a way that will make the very best impression. Perhaps you find out the rep does not have a designer that works with corporate identity. Your approach would be to provide the rep with this service so they can offer their clients a better, more complete package. If the rep already has someone that does corporate identity, you could offer to be a "backup" and work

on a referral basis. There are many possibilities. The important thing is to look at what the rep's needs are and how you can fill them. To find listings of reps, look in annual creative sourcebooks. Some, like *The Workbook* (Los Angeles), list the talents represented and the rep's specialties. You can buy a mailing list or directory of reps that belong to SPAR, the Society of Photographer and Artist Reps (New York). SPAR also has a newsletter where you can advertise for a rep for your business. Also, Writer's Digest Books (Cincinnati, Ohio) publishes an annual directory of reps that have responded by survey that they would like to interview additional creative professionals. The *Guide to Literary Agents and Art/Photo Reps* lists reps, the artists or designers they represent, what they want to see in new talent, and how to contact them.

Since more and more emphasis is being placed on marketing tools such as direct mail and advertising and less on the traditional repping methods of "cold-calling," look for a rep with a strong marketing background.

Hire a Marketing Coordinator

The designer as sole proprietor is still the most popular form of design business. However, this does not mean working alone! Today's design business owner may need to employ people to help with the daily chores of marketing and management as an alternative to an independent representative. Before you say, "I can't afford to hire someone," keep an open mind. You can't afford *not* to get help. In the past, you could be just a designer and survive nicely on whatever came in the door. That is no longer true. (An alternative to hiring full time is to share the employment of a marketing coordinator with another studio.) To know exactly what you need a marketing coordinator to do, start developing a job description. As you go through your day, write down the tasks that did not require your personal attention or design skills—tasks you could have delegated. Do this for two weeks. Categorize the tasks into these three areas:

1. Marketing

2. Management

3. Production

Since you would employ the coordinator, the job responsibilities can be broad. Here is how a detailed two-week job description analysis might look.

1. Organize client/prospect database

2. Research new leads/update database

3. Organize materials for portfolios

4. Prepare materials for cost proposals

5. Manage direct mail/mailing house

6. Inventory promo pieces/publicity/tearsheets

7. Keep master calendar of ad design and production

8. Respond to requests from ads/mailings

9. Send/arrange return of traveling and drop-off portfolios

10. Write/mail press releases

11. Handle bookkeeping and filing

12. Update vendor files and samples

Finding the right marketing coordinator is critical. Remember, they will be dealing with your current clients and often are the first encounter with potential clients. The coordinator also will be logging cash disbursements and receipts. This is a really important position, and it is new to the design industry. The short-term pain of an intense search for the right individual will pay off with long-term gain! You can start looking for candidates at local colleges (business departments, of course!); in customer service departments at printers and photo labs (and related businesses); through referrals from your associations; and in the vast and highly qualified pool of early retirees. Pay should be comparable to office or administrative personnel. The greater the client contact, the more money and incentives you should offer. In addition to a salary, you can compensate high-level client contact with salary plus commission.

You could hire someone for as little as fifteen to twenty hours a week at the beginning. This is not only more affordable, it also is easier to find part-time help among students or retirees. Remember to talk to your accountant about financial responsibility and the paperwork involved in becoming an employer.

Yes, it will be hard at first but it will be worth every penny. You are making an investment in your business, in your future!

SUPER STRATEGY

TWENTY-FOUR

Help Clients Help Themselves

"Eight years ago we started with a focus on marketing ourselves to clients as value added but not with added dollars in fees. Then, three years later, we were hired by PepsiCo for a job that changed our firm's direction and relationships with clients. From our previous marketing position, we now provide three divisions or levels of service: (1) Consulting, what we call strategy; (2) Research, developing the audience; and (3) Storytelling, the actual design. We now specialize in internal communications projects for corporations dealing with change. This has allowed us to establish ourselves first as consultants at double or triple normal design fees, and it brings us into the picture much sooner than a traditional design firm. We're selling a completely new design product and have no competition.

"Jensen Communication starts with a very large project built around a major change the company is going through. Then, when the client is happy with that work, they come back with sub-projects for any of our three divisions. Almost all of our clients use the consulting division, which provides jobs for the storytelling division.

"Because of our unique niche marketing position, we are currently working with clients on a regional basis. We are planning national and even international expansion. When you offer a unique service, clients are more likely to use an out-of-town firm."

Bill Jensen
Jensen Communications

Hiring Professional Services

You may at some point feel that the competition for design jobs is so intense you need to hire a rep or a marketing coordinator.

☐ The rep is in a position to help you:
- find new clients.
- keep clients coming back.
- negotiate the best pricing and terms with these clients.

☐ The marketing coordinator is in a position to manage your:
- marketing
- management
- production.

Decide If You Need a Rep

☐ You are ready for a rep if you:
- are too busy to make personal client contacts yourself.
- have enough bread-and-butter work to let you spend the money on the promotional materials a rep will need.
- have a strong style or specialty that a rep can target clients for.
- have enough knowledge about how to sell yourself but want a rep to do it.
- consider yourself first a businessperson and second a designer.
- are willing to spend time assisting the rep, such as creating new samples that the rep needs as selling tools.

- are constantly looking for ways to promote your business but need help.
- practice good business management methods and have a professional attitude toward promotion.
- have a head start on a portfolio of the kind of work you want the rep to get for you.
- have a marketing plan and budget to support your goal(s).

Find the Right Rep

Make sure you understand how the designer/rep relationship works (see page 89). To find a rep, look in annual creative sourcebooks listed on page 93.

Hire a Marketing Coordinator

☐ As an alternative to hiring a rep, consider hiring someone to help with the daily chores of marketing and management. Here are the specific tasks a marketing coordinator can do:
- organize a client/prospect database
- research new leads and update the database
- organize materials for portfolios.
- prepare materials for cost proposals
- manage the direct mail campaigns
- inventory promotional pieces, publicity and tearsheets
- keep a master calendar of ad design and production

- respond to requests from ads and mailings
- send and arrange return of traveling and drop-off portfolios
- write and mail media releases
- handle bookkeeping and filing
- update vendor files and samples

☐ Start your search for a coordinator by contacting:

- the business departments of local colleges
- customer service departments of printers, photo labs and related businesses
- professional association referrals.
- local retiree organizations or networks.

Places to Look for a Representative:

SPAR
Society of Photographer & Artist
Representatives
60 E. 42nd St., Suite 1166
New York, NY 10165
(212) 779-7464

WRITER'S DIGEST BOOKS
Guide to Literary Agents & Art/Photo Reps
1507 Dana Ave.
Cincinnati, OH 45207
(800) 289-0963

THE WORKBOOK
940 N. Highland Ave.
Los Angeles, CA 90038
(213) 856-0008

AMERICAN SHOWCASE
915 Broadway, 14th Floor
New York, NY 10010
(212) 673-6600

BLACK BOOK MARKETING GROUP
866 3rd Ave., 29th Floor
New York, NY 10022
(212) 702-9700

Chapter Eight
Planning for Action

S T E P   O N E
Pull the pieces of
your plan together.

●

S T E P   T W O
Lay out each action.

●

S T E P   T H R E E
Match actions to goals.

●

S T E P   F O U R
Plan action on calendar.

Finally, it's time to pull everything you've learned into a written marketing plan. A written plan is simply a map that will show you how to reach your marketing destination. Also, it will relieve the day-to-day pressure of planning how to find new clients and keep current ones because it includes specific action items. You will cross-reference these action items to your daily calendar (remember chapter one?). As I said in an earlier chapter, this is called "Plan the work, work the plan" to manage both your business and creative areas!

Once you have determined the work you want to do more of (see chapter two), the bulk of the marketing plan will be devoted to deciding how to promote yourself, approaching clients, presenting your talents and following up. These key ingredients all work together as a recipe for your business success, and you'll find that the lack of success will be due to the weakness (or lack of planning) in any one of these areas.

STEP 1 Pull the Plan Together

To ensure actual implementation of your marketing, the Marketing Plan example here includes these parts:

- **Goal**—What you want to achieve.

- **Audience**—To whom you are selling.

- **Timing**—How often you will call, mail, visit new clients.

- **Content**—Consistency of the message. This is very important. Remember, you are marketing what you want to do, not necessarily what you do now!

- **Marketing mix**—The mix of mailings, advertising, publicity and personal selling. You need to determine who (You? A rep?) will make the sales calls.

- **Budget**—The overall marketing budget. Plan on spending an average of 10 percent of projected gross sales for all the materials you'll use for promotion (see chapter two).

In the marketing plan all these components are spelled out in advance. The worst time to make a marketing decision is when you need one!

STEP 2 Lay Out Each Action

This stage of writing your plan is very important and can get out of hand if you don't keep a tight rein. If the item of action is too big or overwhelming, you'll put it off and it probably won't get done. Break down each action into the smallest, most "bite-sized" tasks possible. For example, you might plan to mail your current clients a capabilities brochure for all of your services. Good idea, but too big a "chunk" for scheduling into the day-to-day business of design. Break it down into smaller pieces: develop layout, write copy, get printing estimates. It is not enough to just plan the work, you have to make working the plan possible!

STEP 3 Match Actions to Goals

Be sure each area of the final plan has a clear and reasonable objective. For example, in chapter two we discussed how advertising doesn't sell design, it brings leads that you then can sell to. Publicity won't get people to call, but will influence their reaction when they get your mailing. Be certain your goal for each action is measurable and attainable.

4 Plan Actions on Calendar

Once you have your plan written and every action broken into small pieces, take out your daily calendar or planner and schedule every action item! Never wait to "find" the time for marketing and self-promotion; schedule it. Don't wait to look for assignments when you don't have any. When paying jobs come along, you can always reschedule any action item, such as writing that media release.

SUPER STRATEGY

TWENTY-FIVE

Create a Proactive Plan

"We call our proactive marketing plan 'project creation' because it brings us more work from clients we already have. Here is our six-step strategy: (1) At the initial client meeting, we constantly read between the lines of conversation to pick up clues on the client's target audience, project cost effectiveness, and future projects. (2) We present a proposal for these 'found' projects along with the original job request. (3) We find this multiple project presentation often overcomes the low-budget objection clients have to single projects. Clients find the money when it's for a group of projects. (4) We always try cross-pollination of solutions between different industries. For example, we will propose something successful in the automotive industry for a high-tech client. We find this extra effort creates added value to our project proposal. (5) Every casual conversation, lunch meeting and client contact is carefully monitored for clues to future projects. (6) One of our principals is always involved in the daily project management. Not only do clients love the personal attention, but our ears are more finely tuned for clues to future work."

Drew Haygeman

HIJK

Model Marketing Plan

I. What We Are Selling

This is your marketing goal—the work you want to do more of. It must be consistent throughout all promotions, including concepts for ads and promotions. (See chapter one.)

For example, your goal might be to do more "annual reports and corporate communications promotions; to create projects and meet the needs of corporate clients to communicate and influence the public." It could also be "to provide a solution to a problem a corporation perceives is affecting profits."

Your *action* is to develop six benefits you can offer clients. These benefits will become your selling tools.

Now, use this two-prong approach—objective and action— to complete your plan.

II. Whom We Are Selling To

Corporations that need annual reports: high-end (Fortune 1000) firms and those in the Resort/Hotel/Travel, Computer, Environmental, Health Care and Telecommunications industries.

Action: Subscribe to trade publications for these industries to keep current on industry trends.

III. How We Will Get the Work
A. Direct Mail Campaign

1. Create concept, design and production of campaign.

- Mail every six weeks.

- Use self-mailer with response card.

- Make a strong offer to increase response.

- Preferably use a single, strong message.

- Objective is to "cull" bought mailing lists by getting responses to create personal database.

- Should also work as "miniportfolio" when client is not ready for an appointment.

2. Obtain mailing lists that match target market.
   Action: (1) Order Labels To Go [(212) 673-6600] from American Showcase's database; (2) Call National Register Publishing [(800) 521-8110] for *Standard Directory of Advertisers* database; (3) Call Creative Access [(312) 440-1140]; (4) Check all three of the above lists for the existence of specific corporations by industry.

B. Advertising Campaign

1. Develop concept based on overall objective.

- Objective is to impress and ask for response, and to add corporations to personal database for sales calls.

- Focus on corporate communications with image selection/copy.
Action: Call American Showcase for current media kit [(212) 673-6600].

C. Public Relations Campaign

1. Should reach clients as well as design peers (for referrals).

2. Plan quarterly project releases to all media.

3. Start entering any/all ad/design awards programs with both self-assignment and published work (don't need to win, the judges are often potential clients).

4. Submit work "success stories" to client and industry publications like *Step-By-Step Graphics*.
   Action: (1) Build database of all media, editors of design and advertising industry publications, and all awards programs; (2) Schedule media releases; (3) Review existing work for points three and four.

D. Personal Selling (telemarketing)

1. Concentrate quality time on the "best bets" for commercial assignments and plan monthly or bimonthly calls for follow-up.

- Past clients.

- Past prospects for work.

- Respondents to direct mail and advertising.

- Leads from editorial assignments.

- Leads from mailing lists in strong portfolio area, such as computers.

- Keep list small and manageable. (If you can make twenty calls a week and have a personal database of less than two hundred, you'll be fine with an eight- to ten-week cycle.)

2. Portfolio.

- Continue with laminated transparencies but no larger than 8″ × 10″.

- Need three duplicates of annual report portfolio for traveling.

- Create a multi-industry body of work rather than a specific portfolio.

- Buy new portfolio cases.

3. Promo materials.
   Continue with black folder/ logo/business card but delete editorial work and use ad reprints or laser color copies of images only along with existing PR reprints/bio. (This is now a "capabilities brochure" sent upon request for more information about your firm. Hopefully, other promo pieces can be used here; otherwise, plan on series

of laser color copies of images from annual report portfolio as visuals.)

Action: (1) Build personal database and reorganize portfolio and promo materials; (2) Schedule sales calls and follow-up calls.

Marketing and Promotion Plan

I. What we are selling (our goals).

_____
_____
_____
_____
_____
_____
_____
_____
_____
_____
_____
_____

Action:

_____
_____
_____
_____
_____
_____
_____
_____
_____
_____
_____
_____
_____
_____
_____
_____
_____
_____
_____

II. Whom we are selling to (our target markets).

_____
_____
_____
_____
_____
_____
_____
_____
_____
_____
_____
_____

Action:

_____
_____
_____
_____
_____
_____
_____
_____
_____
_____

III. How we will get the work.

_____
_____
_____
_____
_____
_____
_____

A. Direct mail campaign.

_____
_____
_____
_____

Action:

_____
_____
_____
_____
_____
_____
_____
_____
_____
_____
_____

B. Advertising campaign.

_____
_____
_____
_____
_____
_____
_____
_____
_____
_____

Action:

_____
_____
_____
_____
_____
_____
_____
_____

C. Public relation campaign.

_____
_____
_____
_____
_____
_____
_____
_____

Action:

_____

_____

_____

_____

_____

_____

_____

_____

_____

_____

_____

_____

_____

D. Personal selling (telemarketing).

_____

_____

_____

_____

_____

_____

_____

_____

_____

_____

_____

_____

_____

Action:

_____

_____

_____

_____

_____

_____

_____

_____

_____

_____

_____

Twenty Marketing Tips

1. Check the reference section of your library before buying expensive directories of prospective clients. Check with one of your current clients and ask them to give you one of their out-of-date directories. An older version of these directories is sufficient for your needs because all you need are names and addresses.

2. Find another designer to share the cost of magazine subscriptions or industry directories.

3. Working at home? Make outgoing sales calls on the less-expensive home phone line. This will work only if you can do so in a private and quiet environment.

4. Maximize phone-call time. When you don't get an appointment, ask for a piece of information you can use, such as, who else in the company works with outside designers.

5. Use your personalized company postcards instead of letters for follow-up. It saves time, printing and postage costs.

6. Advertising costs are based on circulation. Consider an ad in an industry association newsletter rather than in a national publication.

7. When considering advertising, it's probably more cost-effective to buy four ¼-page ads over a four-month period than one full-page ad. In other words, frequency is more im-portant than size or even color.

8. Talk to the post office about reducing costs with presorted and bulk-rate mailings. Savings can be substantial if you do a lot of promotional mailings.

9. Investigate laser color copies when you can't afford the more expensive color printing of your portfolio pieces.

10. Well-designed black-and-white or two-color pieces with your name and phone number can be as effective as four-color pieces. Don't wait for the budget to do four-color.

11. Business-card-sized ads, even without illustration, can be used effectively to promote design services.

12. Plan more public relations. It's a form of free advertising. Every time your clients and prospective clients see your name in the local paper or trade journals, it creates recognition and adds credibility.

13. Check into joint-venture printing of promo pieces with printers, color separators, photographers, illustrators and other noncompeting creative professionals.

14. Negotiate with your clients or printers for one or two hundred copies of the brochures you designed and use them as promo pieces by adding your logo label.

15. Join your local design association and negotiate with local art stores and other suppliers for a members-only discount on their services and products.

16. Plan to pursue referrals rather than wait for them.

17. Be sure each promo piece can be used in more than one situation. For example, design postcards that can be used individually in a direct mail campaign, and also together in a cover folder as a miniportfolio.

18. Contact your local business association and offer to trade design services for use of their mailing list in your direct mail campaign.

19. Buying a mailing list from companies like Creative Access (Chicago) can be less expensive than researching and maintaining your own list.

20. Hire a local Girl Scout troop or students to put together your mailings. They can use the extra money (less than it would cost to hire an employee), and you could spend the time more cost-effectively working on your promotions.

SUPER STRATEGY

TWENTY - SIX

The Value of Pro Bono Work

"I have always found that volunteering for pro bono or public service projects has been an important part of my self-promotion strategy. "For the American Cancer Society, I designed a series of invitations titled A Taste For Life. This was a very personal choice of a charity to work with and that is a very important consideration when deciding to do pro bono work. They gave me total design control and paid all the production expenses. Since I was able to handle the printing, I added a press run for personal promos printed without the invitation copy. I was amazed at the amount of attention and projects this brought in from individuals on the American Cancer Society list of over 10,000 people. It turns out that their mailing list included many important corporate clients."

Darlene McElroy
Darlene McElroy Design/Illustration

Chapter Eight Checklist
Planning for Action

Now that you know what kinds of design projects you want to do more of, the kinds of clients you want to contact, and the tools you want to use to contact them, you have to write a plan of action for pulling these elements together and using the tools wisely to achieve your dream.

Pull the Plan Together

Use the guidelines below and the model plan on pages 100-103 to write your own marketing plan.

☐ The first step is to organize the materials you will need to write your marketing and promotion plan. The plan will:
- give you specific action jobs to complete every day.
- be cross-referenced to your daily calendar so you have no excuse for not doing these action jobs.

☐ The parts of the plans are:
- Goal—what you want to achieve.
- Audience—whom you want to sell to.
- Timing—how often you will call, mail or visit.

- Content—your message must be consistent.
- Marketing mix—how you will use and combine direct mail, advertising, publicity and personal selling.
- Budget—Plan on spending an average of 10 percent of your projected gross sales.

Lay Out Each Action

To keep control of the writing process, make sure each action item in your plan is small enough to manage without getting frustrated or overwhelmed.

Match Actions to Goals

Be certain that your goal for each action is measurable and attainable.

Plan Action on Calendar

Schedule each action from your marketing and promotion plan onto your daily calendar. If an action is not on the calendar, most likely it won't get done.

Gallery

Pentagram

•

Lubell • Brodsky

•

Everett Peck

•

Richard Salzman

•

Hornall Anderson

•

Boelts Brothers

•

Pinkard Gill

As you have seen in previous chapters, there are many ways to promote your business. The Gallery section that follows includes both common and unusual examples of both advertising and collateral materials that have proven successful. As you review the Gallery of promotions that follow, I'd like you to consider three key points. First, don't be afraid to be creative. Second, don't be afraid to let your personality show through. And third, schedule time to develop ideas and produce your own promotional materials. Do it today. It worked for every designer represented in this book, and it will work for you!

Pentagram

One of the more unusual promotions presented in the Gallery is an ongoing series of booklets called simply "Pentagram Papers," produced by Pentagram Design, New York, NY. In order to promote themselves, their design style, and their ideas in general, the Pentagram partners frequently run design workshops, lecture to schools and professional organizations, publish books, contribute to exhibitions, and write and design for external and internal publications.

Self-promotional publications, like the Pentagram Papers, are a unique outlet for the partners' creativity. Now in its twenty-first edition, the series is edited by graphic design consultant/partner John McConnell in Pentagram's London office, but different partners have designed different editions. Each one presents an achievement, a curiosity or an idea which has caught the partners' imagination, usually an esoteric subject that would not necessarily find its way into a commercial publication.

The Papers are published about once a year and are used to contact friends, clients and potential clients when a commercial approach would be inappropriate.

Lubell • Brodsky

For advertising and design that's right on the nose...

A more traditional example of promotional material is this four-color capabilities brochure produced by Lubell • Brodsky • Inc. To simplify both bindery and mailing, it is printed two-sides, on a single sheet of 11″ × 17″ glossy stock and then folded to fit in a standard #10 envelope for mailing.

Copy illustrates their philosophy, which is to "promote our client's message, rather than our own graphic style." This allows them to produce a broad range of work for an unusually diverse group of clients, including corporate publishing, real estate, manufacturing, retail stores and educational groups. Awards are mentioned. Photos are simply examples of their work . . . sort of a miniportfolio presentation.

Also, they've included a slogan which pretty much says it all: "For advertising and design that's right on the nose. . . ."

We've done many real estate brochures, for both residential and commercial projects. These two are for recent co-op conversions.

Six representative brochures supplying in-depth technical information to consumers, from a series of more than 50 produced for J.C. Penney.

An employee education and information program which was distributed to all units of American Express Company.

Part of a very large series of teaching guides and workbooks designed for Scholastic, Inc.

In addition to designing packaging for consumer products, we've also created containers, as well as contents, for many sponsored educational kits.

An ongoing campaign of small space ads created for an upscale Brooklyn discount store. They run in New York Magazine and The New York Times.

Everett Peck

Like many successful designers and illustrators, Everett Peck works with an artists representative, Richard Salzman, to promote his business. Everett Peck also advertises. His full-page B&W ad promotes his free for the asking, "ITV—Ten TV Shows I'd like to See" booklet.

The booklet illustrates his creativity and also has a strong call for action on the back cover. It says, "Please contact Richard Salzman for Everett Peck's commercial portfolio (even if you're not a television mogul)."

The entire promotion consists of a B&W ad offering a free booklet, which in turn promotes a look at Everett's commercial portfolio. Notice that both the ad and booklet are B&W. It costs much less to produce than four-color. Media insertions are also less expensive, which allows higher frequency. A B&W ad run four to six times per year will yield a greater response than a four-color ad you can only afford to run once or twice.

Richard Salzman

Richard Salzman is a very successful artists representative who, among other things, throws an annual Memorial Day party to help promote his business. In order to get portfolio presentations, Richard also produces a co-op brochure titled "Natural Resources" featuring illustrations from the artists he represents.

This brochure is noteworthy because it is printed entirely on recycled paper provided by his co-op partner, the Fox River Paper Company. The brochure is distributed to Fox River's mailing list and is direct mailed to five thousand existing and prospective clients for Richard Salzman's artists.

"Natural Resources" has been effective as a company image brochure and has won several awards of excellence in both national and international shows.

Hornall Anderson

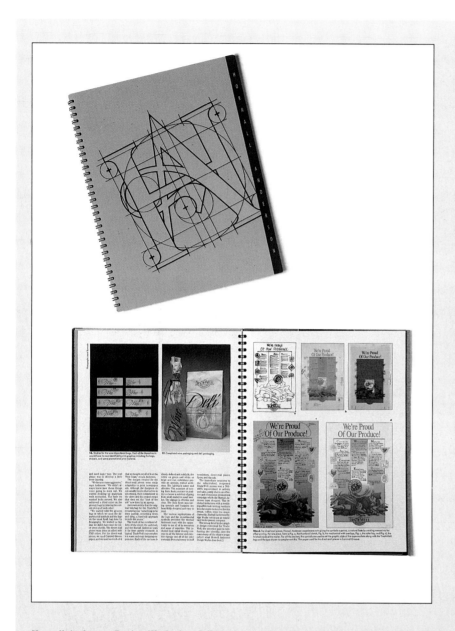

Hornall Anderson Design Works is a full-service graphic design firm that believes in building partnership relationships with its clients. They specialize in corporate, brand and product identity; packaging and merchandising materials; annual reports and collateral materials; and signage, exhibits, and a variety of promotional programs.

In order to educate and inform potential clients regarding their broad capabilities, they have produced a brochure titled "Introduction to Hornall Anderson Design Works." This informative piece provides background information on firm history, their approach to graphic design, and a client list which includes Airborne Express, Holland America, Food Services of America, K2 Corporation and Starbucks Coffee Company.

To add credibility, the brochure also includes a section devoted to reprinted articles on their firm, which is followed by a sample of firm projects and case histories. Once again, this is a fine example of a sincere, straightforward concept that has proven to be instrumental in new business development.

Boelts Brothers

Jack and Eric Boelts of Boelts Brothers Design place a great deal of emphasis on regional, local and national design competitions. In fact, they have used money budgeted for local advertising to enter competitions which they feel are more effective than traditional advertising avenues.

What do they enter in competitions? Innovative promotions that work. One notable promotion was titled "Missing With Your Advertising Plan?" It was designed to encourage advertisers to select and place ads in a special section of *AOPA Pilot* magazine called "Turbine Pilot," which offers a low cost-per-thousand and high-quality readership.

They also designed a promotion to showcase selected statistics of the *AOPA Pilot* reader audience. They produced a poster titled "Where All Your Dollars Make Sense" and designed a series of direct mail gifts preceded by a teaser postcard. They also sent four real dollar bills, uncut, from the U.S. Treasury Department. Numerous people called and asked if the bills were real—if they could cut them apart, etc.

Enter promotions like these in competition, and you will develop a reputation for clever promotions that work. Leads for new business and new clients will follow.

Pinckard Gill

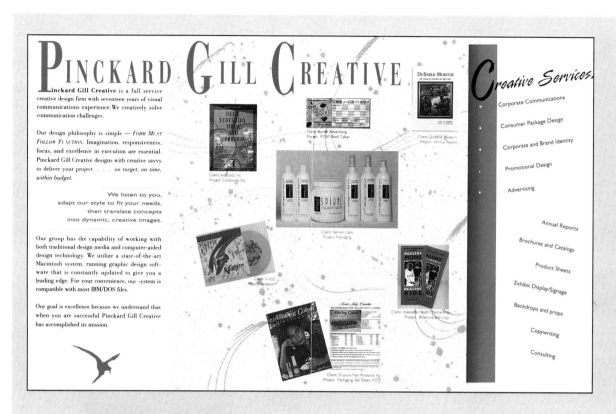

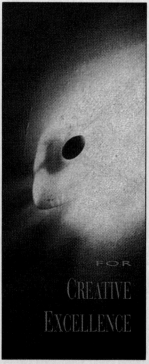

Pinckard Gill Creative is a full-service graphic design firm that specializes in corporate communications and consumer packaging with seventeen years experience. Their design philosophy is "form follows function."

In order to come up with a concept for their capabilities brochure, they looked at their clients and the type of work they were doing versus the type of clients and work they wanted to do. They also thought about what makes them different from other design firms and about why they design the way they do.

As a result, new objectives were defined. Their brochure was designed to meet these new objectives and also to reflect their style. As is common, their brochure folds down to fit in a #10 envelope for ease of mailing.

The thought behind this brochure is "what is important." They began the creative process after they established their new objectives. And this is exactly the way you should proceed with your promotional pieces.

Index

More Great Books for Knock-Out Graphic Design